The U...
Scottish C
Coast to Coast Acro...

EXCELLENT BOOKS

www.excellentbooks.co.uk
richardpeacecycling.com
richardpeace6@gmail.com
First edition printed 2015
ISBN 978 1901464 32 0

CONTENTS

ROUTE TOTALS
ANNAN - FORTH BRIDGE OPTION 201 km 125 miles
ANNAN-DUMFRIES-FORTH BRIDGE OPTION 233.5 km 144.5 miles
Note The route to the sea at Musselburgh is 170.5 km / 106 miles

Rural bliss on a very quiet road through the Moorfoot Hills.

Scottish C2C and surrounding cycle network - Southern Scotland

SC2C	Scottish Sea to Sea (201km / 125mi)
68	National Cycle Network with route number (green background = off road)
10	Regional routes (some routes numbered with blue and white signs)
——	Other traffic free route
——	Suggested minor road route
- - -	Train line with selected stations in red

miles 0 — 10
km 0 — 16

The Scottish C2C – Solway Firth to the Forth Bridge

The route

Launched in 2014, the Scottish C2C is the brainchild of the founders of the original runaway success story that is the C2C cycle route across the north of England between Whitehaven and Sunderland - David Gray and John Grimshaw CBE.

A route for all, the Scottish C2C includes gentle railpaths, nearly deserted roads through wild glens and some lovely waterside stretches. Towns are small and cyclist friendly and Edinburgh's cycling provision is good. There's opportunity to stop off at three of the 7 Stanes mountain biking trail centres and other attractions along the way are many and varied.

Signed and mapped, all major route sections are identified by the distinctive Scottish C2C sign and there are also spurs and route options often using parts of Sustrans' National Cycle Network.

Although the route is in its infancy, it has a number of options which offer a choice between on and off road, direct or meandering and scenic or even more scenic! Some options are well endowed with accommodation and refreshment stops, others less so. The future is likely to bring further route options and increase the amount of traffic free path available, with further accommodation and refuelling stops cropping up, no doubt.

The harbour in Annan is a good starting point; it's easily accessible from the town and has plenty of space for vehicles to disgorge bikes and riders. Though not as bustling as it would once have been, revamp plans may well give it a fillip. Another possible start point is the site of the former Solway Viaduct, by the sea to the south-east of Annan centre.

All roads now lead to Moffat. The main Scottish C2C route goes north from Annan to pass through rich, undulating farmland past Lockerbie, crossing the motorway north of Johnstonebridge to roll into popular Moffat. The roads are quiet with gentle hills and attractive scenery. There is little on the route

You're on quiet roads over gentle gradients most of the way from Annan to Moffat. Here the route is signed alongside local route 11 near Annan.

itself in the way of facilities but Ecclefechan and Lockerbie are close by and to the west Lochmaben is an attractive visit.

The western route option (not signed as the Scottish C2C but as National Cycle Route 7 and regional route 10) goes down the coast and alongside the River Nith to Dumfries before heading through the hilly Forest of Ae to Moffat. It's a route of two halves certainly, being in the main level, leisurely and on road up to Dumfries and in the main hilly, challenging and off road thereafter.

The Moffat to Peebles section offers on and off road options, sweeping through the Annan valley to the dizzying heights of the Devil's Beef Tub.

Hilly and sometimes rocky; the Forest of Ae

From there a fast road descent from the route's highest point takes you down the Tweed valley and into Peebles. In time there may be a full traffic free alternative down the valley to join the recently opened Tweed Valley Railway Path between Peebles and Innerleithen.

The road route to the south of this path is also a delight. You're in mountain biking country with the Glentress centre just east of Peebles. The route itself is a tarmac traffic free breeze from Peebles to Innerleithen.

High quality traffic free railpath from Peebles to Innerleithen

From Innerleithen only the Moorfoot Hills stand between you and the Edinburgh hinterland, a steady up and an exhilarating down leading to a panoramic view over the plain and the city. From here you drop down and head through Dalkeith and are now on largely traffic free paths all the way to the Forth Bridge. There are many splendid sections along Portobello promenade, the Leith railway paths, the Granton esplanades and the estate roads past Dalmeny House, which bring you to the piers of the Forth rail bridge – 125 miles from the start.

Route surface and signage

All the roads between towns are light on traffic. The A701 Moffat to Peebles section is actually usually fairly lightly trafficked and in any case the ultimate route aim is to make an off road option available using wind farm access roads and a railpath along the Tweed Valley.

Railpaths at Dumfries and between Peebles and Innerleithen are tarmac and probably some of the best examples you'll find in the country. The off road routes through the Forest of Ae and up the Annan valley north of Moffat can, in places, be steep with rough surfaces and are probably more easily accomplished on a mountain bike.

Off road sections like this one north of Moffat can be bypassed by alternative tarmac routes.

Smooth tarmac with little or no motor traffic makes up the majority of the Scottish C2C

Navigation should be fairly straightforward. At road junctions there are C2C stickers on the posts of traffic signs or occasionally C2C stencils on the road surface. The off road sections have signs on gateposts or at other roadside locations. Overall, don't expect to see signs or waymarking on long, junctionless stretches but do expect to find it at junctions.

Main traffic free bike trails used by the Scottish Coast to Coast

Trail	From	To	Surface	Length km / miles
Through Dumfries	Kingholm Quay	Locharbriggs	Tarmac	10 / 6
Forest of Ae	Ae village	Earshaig	Unsealed forest track (can be rocky), often hilly	18 / 11
Track above Annandale	Ericstane	A701 near Devil's Beef Tub	Rough hilly farm track; can be muddy and stony	1.5 / 0.9
Tweed Valley railpath	Peebles	Innerleithen	Smooth tarmac	9 / 5.5
Esk Valley paths	Dalkeith	Musselburgh	Smooth tarmac	8 / 5
Forth Promenade paths (uses John Muir Way for short section at Musselburgh and after Cramond).	Musselburgh	Forth Bridge	Smooth tarmac	22.5 / 14
Brunstane Path & Innocent Railpath (Edinburgh centre option)	Musselburgh	Innocent Rail Tunnel	Smooth tarmac	6.5 / 4

What kind of bike?

Like the English C2C, the route does contain several long climbs and some of the off road options have sections of rough surface, but careful selection of alternatives should allow just about any type of bike to complete the ride. Road racing bikes, tricycles, bike trailers and tandems are probably as well not using the Ae Forest and the off road option north of Moffat. If hill climbing isn't your bag anyway, perhaps look at using an electric bike.

Sustrans and the National Cycle Network (NCN)

Sustrans is a leading UK charity enabling people to travel by foot, bike or public transport for more of the journeys they make every day and, although the Scottish C2C has been devised independently of Sustrans it uses several sections of the Sustrans NCN.

Currently the NCN consists of over 14,000 miles of signed cycling and walking routes on traffic free paths and quiet roads across the UK.

Created from one of the first ever National Lottery grants in 1995, the popularity of the Network has grown enormously and it now carries over a million walking and cycling journeys daily and passes within a mile of 57% of the population.

The maintenance and the development of the National Cycle Network and Sustrans' other projects rely on the kind donations of Sustrans supporters. **Make your move and support Sustrans today!** Visit www.sustrans.org.uk or call 0845 838 0651 to find out more.

The Scottish C2C also uses several sections of local or regional routes and these are detailed below along with the NCN sections used.

Route	From	To
Local route 11	Annan	Beyond Brydekirk
NCN 7	Annan (western option)	Dumfries (western option)
Regional Route 10	Dumfries	Moffat
Borders Loop & Regional Route 82	A701 near the Talla Reservoir (includes part of optional road route if not using the Peebles to Innerleithen railpath)	Innerleithen
NCN 1	Innerleithen	Dalkeith (optional use on to Musselburgh)
NCN 1	Cramond (quicker but less scenic route option, not signed as Scottish C2C)	Forth Bridge
NCN 76 (Round the Forth route)	Cramond	Forth Bridge (route end)

For a summary of the complex network of NCN routes around Edinburgh see pages 104-5.

How long should I take?

Three or four days should allow you to complete the route in a reasonably leisurely fashion with perhaps a little time out for rest periods and a bit of sightseeing. However, there's enough along and near the route to make a good touring holiday, really of whatever length of time you wish. If it's a sporting challenge on a fast bike, 24 hours or less may well do it.

When should I go?

If you can hit the road at short notice, just study the weather forecasts and act accordingly. The areas the route passes through are not notorious for any extremes of weather; in fact, for Scotland, they're amongst the more temperate areas with statistically the best of the sunshine, peaking in May and June, and good long summer days. In June you can expect around seventeen and a half hours of daylight, that's about an hour more than you'd get in London at that time of year.

The wettest months are September to January. If you're coming from outside Scotland and prefer to avoid school holidays, bear in mind that Scottish school holidays can differ to the rest of the UK, the summer holidays in particular starting and finishing a couple of weeks or so earlier than the rest of the country. If you would like to couple your C2C adventure with other diversions, the annual Tweedlove Bike Festival in May / June time is a fortnight of bike events for all kinds of riders. The Edinburgh Festival and the Fringe festival take place in August each year. The area as a whole offers activities ranging from golf and fly fishing to mountain biking and music festivals, spa treatments and fine dining to hot air ballooning, but if you just want to sit quietly and enjoy the scenery, there are boundless opportunities.

Seasonal route fruit!

Riding Information & Advice

This guide should give you all the information you need to complete the route but do keep an eye on **chain-events.co.uk** for route updates. They also run guided, supported tours along the route, courtesy of route co-founder David Gray.

Bikes are welcome on Scotrail trains, here at Dumfries station

Travel Information

Annan is not difficult to get to. Lying on the north coast of the Solway Firth it's about half an hour by road from the M74. On the train from Glasgow it's a couple of hours or so, from Newcastle on a direct service the same and from Carlisle about twenty minutes. Edinburgh services change at Glasgow or Carlisle and mostly take nearer three hours. None of the operating companies charge for carrying bikes but space can be limited. Scotrail and Northern Rail do not offer reservations on these lines but Virgin require them (telephone 03445 56 56 50) so if you're planning a rail return from Edinburgh, preparation may be needed. Folded, bagged folding bikes travel as luggage.

Accommodation Listings and Contacts

The listings in the guide shown with blue numbering have been chosen because they are near the route.

There are several national organisations that also offer accommodation or listings services that might prove useful:

Beds for Cyclists **bedsforcyclists.co.uk**

Camping and Caravanning Club **campingandcaravanningclub.co.uk**

Visit Britain **visitbritain.com**

Youth Hostels Association **yha.org.uk**

Independent Hostel Guide **independenthostelguide.co.uk**

In general, outside of peak times in the very busiest spots, accommodation shouldn't be a problem but a bit of preparation is certainly advisable. The southern end of the route passes through a popular holiday area which means whilst accommodation is plentiful it can fill up at traditional holiday times, likewise at Festival time in Edinburgh. Some places, campsites as well as guest houses, may have minimum stay requirements at peak periods, although where this applies to guide listings we have tried to give this information. Hotel and b & b accommodation is plentiful in the towns and in Edinburgh but not for the most part in between. Camping requires planning ahead as most of the campsites are near the southern sections of the route and there is only one campsite by the route at the Edinburgh end, although the city is well endowed with hostels.

The listings in the guide are near the route but particularly in the towns and in Edinburgh more options are obviously available if you are happy to travel a bit away from the route.

There are some stunning campsites en route, here at Powfoot

Future Route Development

The former railway lines of Upper Tweeddale in the Scottish Borders have huge potential as walking, cycling and horseriding routes; many users already enjoy the new high quality tarmac traffic free path between Peebles and Innerleithen.

The aim of the Upper Tweed Railway Paths organisation is to extend this route west, connecting Peebles to Broughton, Biggar, Symington and Tweedsmuir. An initial feasibility study was an essential first step and UTRP appointed consultants John Grimshaw CBE and David Gray. John was founder, Director and Chief Engineer of Sustrans, and now works freelance to establish successful multiuse paths. David is known for conceiving and developing the popular C2C route, from Whitehaven to Sunderland. Input also came from Vyv Wood-Gee whose experience of route development in Southern Scotland includes the recently developed Annandale Way.

For the Scottish C2C this means plans are afoot to extend the traffic free route west of Peebles to Lyne Station and back up the Tweed Valley, initially as far as the Crook Inn.

The former railway line up the Tweed Valley has a fascinating history. The eight mile spur was built up a remote Borders hillside for the sole purpose of building Talla Reservoir – the line disappeared just 15 years later. A 300-strong workforce, including many Irish navvies, moved more than 100,000 tonnes of puddle clay (clay, gravel and sand mixture) needed to seal water in the reservoir. Existing roads were unsuitable to move so much. Work started in 1895 on the line, which branched off south from Broughton.

The trackbed of the old Talla Reservoir line seen in the Upper Tweed Valley. Upper Tweed Railway Paths aims to bring it back to life for cyclists, walkers and horseriders.

© Duncan Davidson

The line included a 100ft steel bridge whose abutments used granite from Italy and also a platform stop at the Crook Inn (licensed since 1604 and once owned by the contractors who built Talla Reservoir, who laid on a Friday night train for navvies, so getting the wages they paid them straight back!). In recent years this historic coaching inn has been saved from residential redevelopment and bought by the local community. There are plans to reopen, keeping it as a pub but also providing accommodation and a community hub. The Paddy was the name of the train that once bought Irish workers there; so rowdy was their behaviour a police station was built nearby.

The puddle clay was moved to the base of the reservoir via an aerial ropeway named after famed tightrope walker "Blondin" (Jean-François Gravelet) who crossed Niagara Falls. 1905 saw the whole project finished and though there was a desire to retain the railway for passenger trains between Broughton and Tweedsmuir the line's rails were sold in 1910. Today water from Talla, Edinburgh's most distant reservoir, is still transported using gravity through a 35 mile network of pipes and tunnels, crossing seven valleys to reach treatment works at Glencorse on the south side of the city.

Upper Tweed Railway Paths

www.uppertweedrailwaypaths.org.uk
Please sign up as a supporter to receive our occasional e-news
Registered Scottish charity SC044987

Looking down the Talla Reservoir
© Duncan Davidson

View over the River Annan
between Millhousebridge
and Johnstonebridge

Annan ~ Moffat

From the handsome town of Annan there are two starting points; the old harbour, or the former site of the incredible railway crossing of the Solway Firth. Whilst the old harbour is the nearest to town, the Seafield Farm option is the most spectacular, with sweeping views across the Solway Firth to northern Lakeland, salmon nets standing along the sands at low tide, the foreshore often speckled with birdlife.

Navigation is a little confusing in Annan itself due to a plethora of other signed routes but once into the countryside things are more straightforward and you will have many miles of beautiful, quiet country lanes to yourself as you shadow the Annan valley all the way to Moffat.

Route Info

Distance 51.5 km (32 miles)

Off road 2.75 km (1.7 miles) This is unsegregated cycle lane (i.e. painted on the road) on a short section of NCN74 that uses the B7076.

Terrain Gently undulating sums up the majority of this section as you head up gentle Annandale, surrounded by rolling agricultural country. Gradients increase slightly after crossing the A74(M) just after Johnstonebridge but the real climbing begins after Moffat over the round masses of the Southern Uplands which can be seen in the distance from this section.

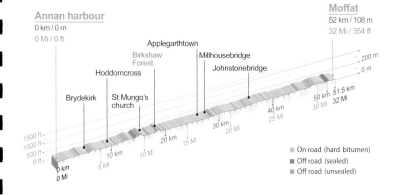

Annan harbour
0 km / 0 m
0 Mi / 0 ft

Moffat
52 km / 108 m
32 Mi / 354 ft

Brydekirk
Hoddomcross
St Mungo's church
Birkshaw Forest
Applegarthtown
Millhousebridge
Johnstonebridge

200 m
0 m

1500 ft
1000 ft
500 ft
0 ft

0 km
0 Mi
5 Mi
10 km
10 Mi
20 km
15 Mi
30 km
20 Mi
25 Mi
40 km
30 Mi
50 km
51.5 km
32 Mi

■ On road (hard bitumen)
■ Off road (sealed)
■ Off road (unsealed)

What to See & Do

• Despite the current rather dilapidated state of the old harbour (restoration underway at the time of writing that will include cycle route map, seating and binoculars for birdwatching) **Annan** has a handsome high street, dominated by its flamboyantly architectural Town Hall. Lots of good eating and / or drinking spots including the Bluebell Inn, Del Amitris and Meganos. The site of the former **Solway Viaduct** that spanned the estuary between Bowness and Annan is a stunningly beautiful alternative start.

• There are two **Scottish national heroes** who were based in the area you ride through. You are in the heart of **Robert Burns** country - one of the Scottish dialect poet's local monikers was Robden of Solway Firth. There are statues of Burns in many towns throughout this area of south-west Scotland. In 2009 he was chosen as the greatest Scot in a Scottish TV vote. Perhaps his best known work remains a musical version of his poem Auld Lang Syne.

Robert the Bruce (Robert I of Scotland 1306-1329) fought not only the mighty and ruthless Edward I of England but rival Scots factions before ascending the Scottish throne. But most famous was his victory over Edward II at Bannockburn. He would have stayed at Lochmaben castle during his youth. There is a statue of the Bruce on Annan town hall.

• There are several interesting **churches** along the way. There are gothic-feeling ruins at Hoddomcross and St Mungo's (take a look at the many memorial plaques) and Applegarthtown - a beautifully kept church with enormous gravestones outside and a lovely green in front with war memorial. A great picnic / drinks stop.

• **Lochmaben** You can detour down the busy, fast A709 past beautiful Castle Loch to this pretty little town with local services including bakery, hotels and a campsite.

Gently undulating, virtually traffic free roads take you along much of Annandale

Moffat's beautiful rural setting

• At **Dryfesdalegate Farm** the route passes a 16th century battlesite where the clan Maxwell army was almost exterminated by the clan Johnstone. Longstanding clan hatred came to a head after the theft of a horse and tit-for-tat reprisals escalated, leading to a battle involving well over 2,000 men and the involvement of James VI of Scotland (later James I of England).

• **Moffat** has a lovely broad, handsome main street lined by some fine buildings and charming narrow back streets of brightly painted stone cottages. It's no surprise part of the town is an official Conservation Area. There is a local museum, riverside walks and plenty of attractive eateries and accommodation, partly the result of Moffat being a major stopover for those travelling further north. Look out for the world's narrowest hotel and Scotland's shortest street and its oldest chemists; Moffat claims them all! Other attractive local spots include Station Park and the Old Well Theatre. There's also a great range of individual pubs and eateries.

Nearby:
• Pretty little **Ecclefechan** is best known as the birthplace of Thomas Carlyle, most famous for his dramatic historical account of the French Revolution.

• **Lockerbie** is a small market town of red sandstone, its centre dominated by the town hall's ornate clock tower.
Lockerbie Manor lies just to the north of the town. Once the home of the Marquis of Queensberry, said to have come up with the rules of boxing in his dining room here. It is now an outdoor activity centre and offers family breaks during school holiday periods.

For Annan to Dumfries see following chapter pg 35.

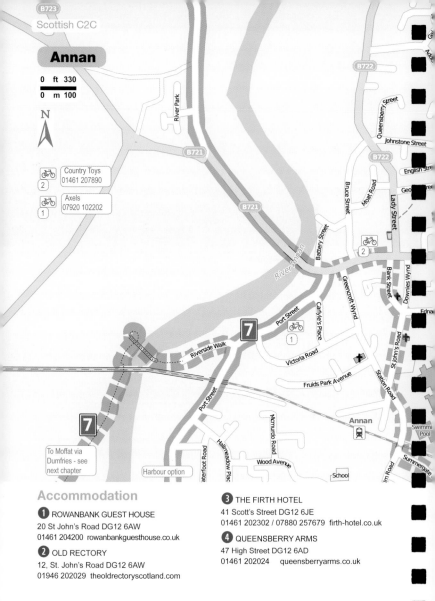

Annan

0 ft 330
0 m 100

N

Country Toys
01461 207890
2

Axels
07920 102202
1

B723

B722

Queensberry Street

Johnstone Street

B722

English Stre

Geo

Bruce Street

Moat Road

Lady Street

Battery Street

Bank Street

Downies Wynd

Edna

River Annan

River Park

B721

B721

Greencroft Wynd

Carlyle's Place

Port Street

St John's Road

7

Riverside Walk

Victoria Road

Fruids Park Avenue

Station Road

7

Port Street

Mcmurdo Road

Hallmeadow Plac

aterfoot Road

Wood Avenue

Annan

Swimmi
Pool

Summergate

n Road

School

To Moffat via
Dumfries - see
next chapter

Harbour option

Accommodation

1 ROWANBANK GUEST HOUSE
20 St John's Road DG12 6AW
01461 204200 rowanbankguesthouse.co.uk

2 OLD RECTORY
12, St. John's Road DG12 6AW
01946 202029 theoldrectoryscotland.com

3 THE FIRTH HOTEL
41 Scott's Street DG12 6JE
01461 202302 / 07880 257679 firth-hotel.co.uk

4 QUEENSBERRY ARMS
47 High Street DG12 6AD
01461 202024   queensberryarms.co.uk

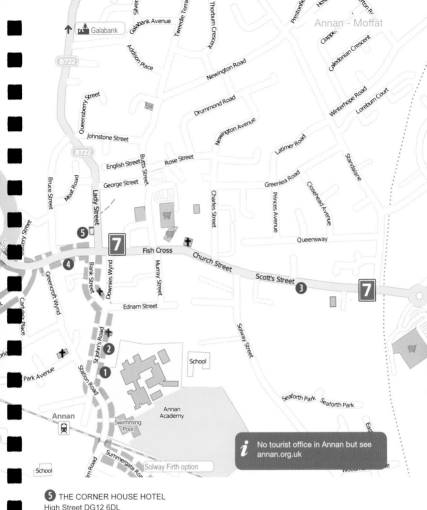

5 THE CORNER HOUSE HOTEL
High Street DG12 6DL
01461 202754 thecornerhousehotel.com

For route directions see overleaf

Directions

There are two recommended start points:

If you want to dip your wheel in the water start at the old harbour (now partly disused) found at the end of Port Street **1a**. Head away from the port up Port Street to the High Street and left (town centre to the right).

The most picturesque starts by the old viaduct abutment at Seafield Farm **1b**. From here just follow the road to gradually climb and just after passing under an old railway bridge go left onto Annerley Road. At the end of Annerley Road turn right then right again at the next T-junction to pass Annan train station. Descend to the roundabout by the swimming pool and straight across. Bear left down Bank Street to come to the High Street and head left along it.

Both start options join at the Bluebell Inn at the end of the High Street. Carry on to cross over the bridge then take first right signed Brydekirk (also signed cycle route 11). Pass the cemetery on the right (commonwealth war graves here). Follow this road for 2.6km (1.6 miles), ignoring any minor turnings, and meet the High Street in Brydekirk **2** and turn right. Pass the Brig Inn and cross the river.

After a steady climb out of Brydekirk lovely views over the Annan valley reveal themselves. At a crossroads **3** head left for Ecclefechan (Eaglesfield straight on).

6 THE WATERSIDE ROOMS
Dornock Brow House, Dornock DG12 6SX
01461 40232 thewatersiderooms.co.uk

GALABANK CARAVAN AND CAMPSITE
North Street, Annan DG12 5DQ
01461 203539 May to September

Annan seen from the route out of town

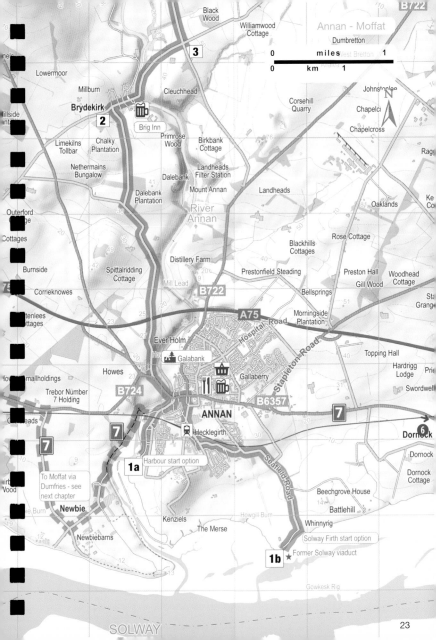

B722

Black Wood

Williamwood Cottage

Dumbretton

West Bretton

3

miles 1

km 1

Lowermoor

Millburn

Brydekirk

2

Brig Inn

Cleuchhead

Corsehill Quarry

Johnstonlee

Chapelci

Chapelcross

Rag

Limekilns Tollbar

Chalky Plantation

Primrose Wood

Birkbank Cottage

Nethermains Bungalow

Dalebank

Landheads Filter Station

Mount Annan

Landheads

Oaklands

Ke Co

Dalebank Plantation

River Annan

Outerford ige

Cottages

Burnside

Corrieknowes

Spittalridding Cottage

Distillery Farm

Mill Lead

Prestonfield Steading

Blackhills Cottages

Rose Cottage

Preston Hall

Gill Wood

Woodhead Cottage

Bellsprings

Sta Grange

Morningside Plantation

B722

A75

Hospital Road

Topping Hall

Ever Holm

Galabank

Gallaberry

Stapleton Road

Hardrigg Lodge

Prie

Swordwell

Howes

B724

Trebor Number 7 Holding

7

ANNAN

Hecklegirth

B6357

7

Dornock

6

Dornock

7

Harbour start option

1a

Dornock Cottage

To Moffat via Dumfries - see next chapter

Newbie

Newbiebarns

Kenziels

The Merse

Howgill Burn

Whinnyrig

Beechgrove House

Battlehill

Solway Firth start option

1b ★ Former Solway viaduct

Gowkesk Rig

SOLWAY

23

Soon after crossing a small bridge turn left at the fork **4** (keeping right here will take you to Ecclefechan) following route 11 signs.

Coming into Hoddomcross pass the ruined church and graveyard **5** and head straight over at the crossroads, signed Lockerbie B723. At the next T-junction turn right joining the B723, signed Kettleholm and Lockerbie. TAKE CARE Fast traffic on the B723. After around 2km (1.2 miles) on the B723 turn left **6** signed Dalton 4 and Middleshaw. Descend and cross the tiny Water of Milk.

7 ECCLEFECHAN HOTEL
High Street, Ecclefechan DG11 3DF
01576 300213 ecclefechanhotel.co.uk

8 KIRKCONNEL HALL HOTEL
Ecclefechan DG11 3JH
01576 300277
www.kirkconnelhallhotel.co.uk
 also offered

CRESSFIELD CARAVAN PARK
Townfoot Ecclefechan DG11 3DR
01576 300702
cressfieldpark.com

HODDOM CASTLE CARAVAN & CAMPING PARK
Hoddom DG11 1AS
01576 300251 hoddomcastle.co.uk

If arriving by bike from England you will have to change at Carlisle, whatever direction you come from, for the 20 minute hop using the **Scotrail** service to Annan.

If so it's likely you will use **Northern Rail** for at least the last part of the journey as they provide local trains thoughout the north of England (for example the popular Newcastle-Carlisle service). Their quoted policy is 'Bikes are carried free of charge at any time and you don't need to make reservations. Space is allocated on a first come, first served basis. We can only carry a maximum of two bikes per train but conductors .... have the right to refuse entry if the train is busy.' Tandems and other 'non-standard' bikes are likely to be excluded.

First TransPennine Express also use the East Coast main line and carry bikes free with reservations being made 24 hours plus in advance by calling 0845 600 1674.

Virgin run lots of trains along the West Coast main line running through Carlisle. Bikes are carried free but an advance reservation is needed and you are supplied with a printed label. Ask a station employee in advance where your allotted space is on the train (you'll only have a few minutes to get your bike and gear aboard). We recommend that you reserve a space as early as possible and at least 24 hours before departure

If coming from Scotland, there are direct **Scotrail** services from Glasgow and an Edinburgh Haymarket to Carlisle direct service. Bike carriage is subject to space and, in some cases, to a cycle reservation. Reservations can be made by contacting 0330 303 0111

For all companies folders travel as normal baggage but should be bagged.

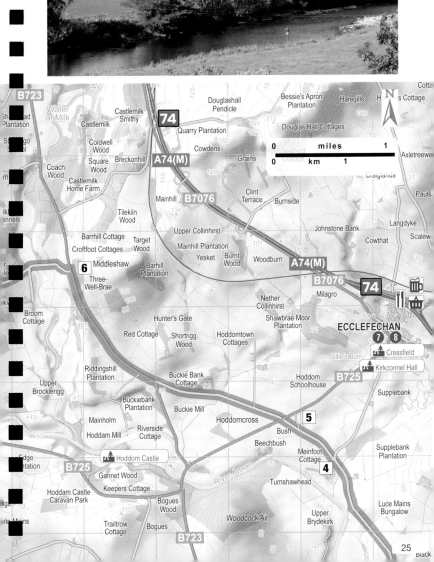

River Annan fishing

B723

Water of Milk

Castlemilk Smithy

Castlemilk

74

Douglashall Pendicle

Bessie's Apron Plantation

Haregills

Cottage

's Cottage

Quarry Plantation

Douglas Hall Cottages

Shad Plantation

Coldwell Wood

Castlemilk

Cowdens

Grains

Newfield Cottage

Axletreewe

St Mungo School

Square Wood

Breckonhill

A74(M)

Craiglands

Pauls

Coach Wood

Castlemilk Home Farm

Mainhill

B7076

Clint Terrace

Burnside

Tilekiln Wood

Upper Collinhirst

Johnstone Bank

Cowthat

Langdyke

Scalew

ki nnels

Barrhill Cottage

Target Wood

Mainhill Plantation

Croftfoot Cottages

Yesket

Burnt Wood

Woodburn

A74(M)

6

Middleshaw

Barhill Plantation

B7076

74

Three-Well-Brae

Nether Collinhirst

Milagro

Broom Cottage

Hunter's Gate

Red Cottage

Shortrigg Wood

Shawbrae Moor Plantation

Hoddomtown Cottages

ECCLEFECHAN
7 **8**

Gillie's Burn

Cressfield

Riddingshill Plantation

Buckie Bank Cottage

Kirkconnel Hall

Upper Brocklerigg

Buckiebank Plantation

Hoddom Schoolhouse

B725

Supplebank

Mainholm

Buckie Mill

Hoddomcross

Bush

5

Riverside Cottage

Beechbush

Supplebank Plantation

Hoddam Mill

Meinfoot Cottage

Edge Plantation

B725

Hoddom Castle

Gannet Wood

Turnshawhead

4

Hoddam Castle Caravan Park

Keepers Cottage

River Annan

Luce Mains Bungalow

ge Mains

Trailtrow Cottage

Bogues Wood

Bogues

Woodcock Air

Upper Brydekirk

B723

black

25

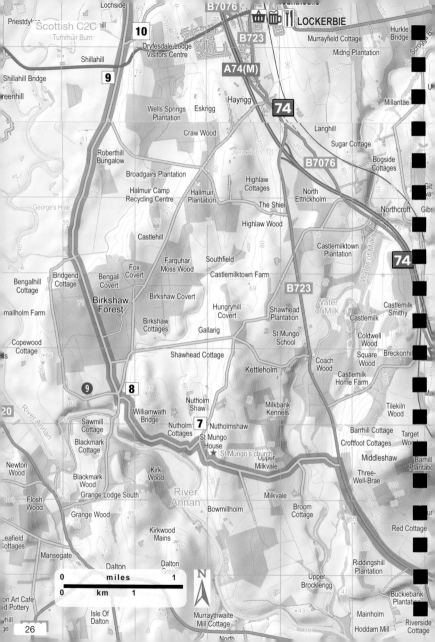

Lochside

B7076

LOCKERBIE

Scottish C2C
Tummuir Burn

10

Dryfesdale Lodge
Visitors Centre

B723

Murrayfield Cottage

Hurkle
Bridge

Midrig Plantation

Shillahill

A74(M)

Priestdykes

Millantae

Shillhill Bridge

9

eenhill

greenhill

Wells Springs
Plantation

Eskrigg

Hayrigg

74

Craw Wood

Langhill

Sugar Cottage

Roberthill
Bungalow

Junction 18

B7076

Bogside
Cottages

Broadgairs Plantation

Highlaw
Cottages

Halmuir Camp
Recycling Centre

Hallmuir
Plantation

North
Ettrickholm

The Shiel

Northcroft

Gibs

George's Hole

Highlaw Wood

74

Castlehill

Castlemilktown
Plantation

Water of Milk

Farquhar
Moss Wood

Southfield

Fox
Covert

Bengall
Covert

Castlemilktown Farm

Castlemilk
Smithy

Bridgend
Cottage

Bengahill
Cottage

Birkshaw Covert

Water
of Milk

Birkshaw
Forest

Hungryhill
Covert

Shawhead
Plantation

Castlemilk

smallholm Farm

Birkshaw
Cottages

Gallarig

St Mungo
School

Coldwell
Wood

Breckonhi

Copewood
Cottage

Shawhead Cottage

Square
Wood

s

Coach
Wood

Castlemilk
Home Farm

9

8

Kettleholm

River Annan

20

Sawmill
Cottage

Williamwath
Bridge

Nutholm
Shaw

Nutholm
Cottages

7

Nutholmshaw

Milkbank
Kennels

Tilekiln
Wood

Barrhill Cottage

Target
Woo

Blackmark
Cottage

St Mungo
House

St Mungo's church

Croftfoot Cottages

Middleshaw

Barhill
Plantatic

Newton
Wood

Blackmark
Wood

Kirk
Wood

Upper
Milkvale

Three-
Well-Brae

Flosh
Wood

Grange Lodge South

River
Annan

Milkvale

Grange Wood

Bowmillholm

Broom
Cottage

Red Cottage

eafield
ottages

Kirkwood
Mains

Mansegate

Dalton

Dalton
Green

Upper
Brocklerigg

Riddingshill
Plantation

Buckiebank
Plantation

0   miles   1

N

0   km   1

on Art Cafe
d Pottery

26

Isle Of
Dalton

Murraythwaite
Mill Cottage

Mainholm

Hoddam Mill

Riverside
Cottage

North

At the unmarked T-junction **7** turn left to descend to the ruined St. Mungo's church you can see in the valley bottom. Come to a T-junction by a tiny bridge **8** and turn right signed Lockerbie 4.5. Over the bridge ignore right and left and climb and drop gently through Birkshaw Forest. Ignore a tiny left at Bengall farm buildings and a further right signed Kettleholm 3 to come to the A709 **9** and head straight over signed Millhousebridge.

Lockerbie detour Turn next right **10** signed Lockerbie 1/2. Follow over A74M and across B7076 to pick up cycle route sign to town centre onto Leonard Terrace then Livingstone Place, going right on busy Townhead Street to bring you onto Lockerbie High St.

9 RIVERSIDE MILL B&B
Dalton Hook DG11 1DG
01576 510016 riversidemill-lockerbie.co.uk

The atmospheric St Mungo's church

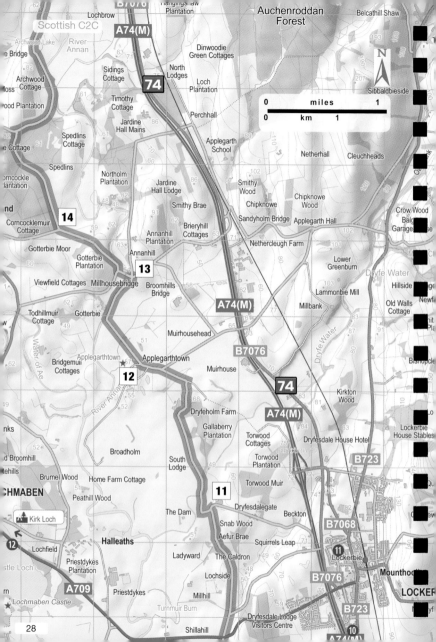

10 SOMERTON HOUSE HOTEL
35, Carlisle Road Lockerbie DG11 2DR
01576 202583 somertonhotel.co.uk

11 QUEENS HOTEL
Old Annan Road Lockerbie DG11 2RB
01576 202415 queenshotellockerbie.co.uk

12 CROWN HOTEL
Bruce Street Lochmaben DG11 1PD
01387 811750 crownhotel-lochmaben.co.uk

KIRK LOCH CARAVAN & CAMPING SITE
Kirk Loch Lochmaben DG11 1PZ
01387 810599 dumgal.gov.uk

Besides the above listings there are lots of other
accommodation options in Lockerbie

11 At the next unmarked T-junction go left and cross the Dryfe Water and through
the farming hamlet of Dryfeholm. Ignore the next right, following signs straight on for
Millhousebridge 1. At the next split **12** Applegarthtown church is marked to the left and
is well worth the short detour, though the route bears right here.
At the crossroads in Millhousebridge **13** turn left signed Templand and Lochmaben and
cross the Annan, taking the next right, signed Templand 1.5.
At the next unmarked split **14** by the forestry plantation bear right. Into the plantation
go right at the unmarked split and come alongside lovely views of the River Annan.

Idyllic Applegarthtown

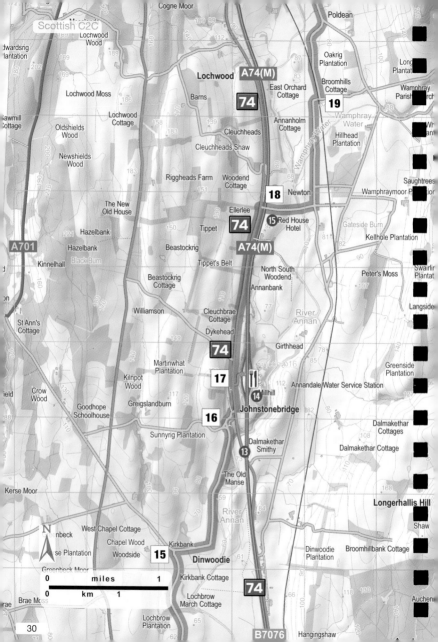

At the T-junction at the tiny hamlet of Kirkbank **15** turn right and follow this road into Johnstonebridge. Right at the T-junction here **16** and drop down to the B7076 where you go left, onto the roadside cycle lanes, now on NCN 74.

Services detour Motorway services (Annandale Water) are shortly signed down to the right **17** (just follow the signs under the M74). The food (Macdonalds, Costa Coffee and WH Smiths) is predictable but there is a nice sitting out area hidden round the back of the building by a small lake.

After 2.8km (1.5 miles) on NCN 74 turn right signed Newton Wamphray **18**, heading over the A74(M). Cross the River Annan and left at the crossroads in the village. Bend right over railway line and immediate left **19**, ignoring the right turn to a church.

13 LOCKERBIE LORRY PARK
Johnstonebridge DG11 2SL
01576 470882 lockerbielorrypark.co.uk

14 DAYS INN
Annandale Water Roadchef
Motorway Service Area A74M DG11 1HD
0844 225 0789 daysinn.co.uk

15 RED HOUSE
Newton Wamphray DG10 9NF
01576 470470 / 0791 918 0841
theredhousebymoffat.co.uk

You briefly join NCN74 between Johnstonebridge and Newton

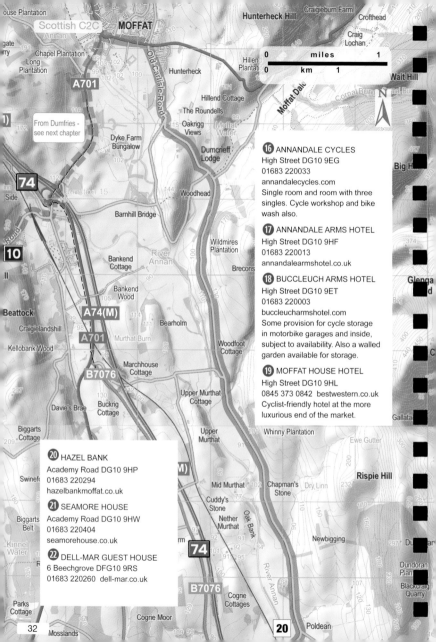

16 ANNANDALE CYCLES
High Street DG10 9EG
01683 220033
annandalecycles.com
Single room and room with three
singles. Cycle workshop and bike
wash also.

17 ANNANDALE ARMS HOTEL
High Street DG10 9HF
01683 220013
annandalearmshotel.co.uk

18 BUCCLEUCH ARMS HOTEL
High Street DG10 9ET
01683 220003
buccleucharmshotel.com
Some provision for cycle storage
in motorbike garages and inside,
subject to availability. Also a walled
garden available for storage.

19 MOFFAT HOUSE HOTEL
High Street DG10 9HL
0845 373 0842   bestwestern.co.uk
Cyclist-friendly hotel at the more
luxurious end of the market.

20 HAZEL BANK
Academy Road DG10 9HP
01683 220294
hazelbankmoffat.co.uk

21 SEAMORE HOUSE
Academy Road DG10 9HW
01683 220404
seamorehouse.co.uk

22 DELL-MAR GUEST HOUSE
6 Beechgrove DFG10 9RS
01683 220260 dell-mar.co.uk

From Dumfries -
see next chapter

20 Turn left at the next T-junction and head through Poldean hamlet. Ignore turnings either side of Moffat Water then and pass the Drumcrieff lodge.
Head into Moffat and meet the A708, going left to use pavement cycle lanes for a short while. Bend right onto the main street.

23 BUCHAN GUEST HOUSE
Beechgrove DG10 9RS
01683 220378
guesthouse-moffat.com

24 QUEENSBERRY HOUSE
12 Beechgrove Moffat DG10 9RS
01683 478341 queensberryhouse.com

25 No. 29 WELL STREET B & B
29 Well Street DG10 9DP
0203 564 2773 no29wellstreetbbmoffat.com

26 LIMETREE HOUSE
Eastgate DG10 9AE
01683 220001 limetreehouse.co.uk
Two night bookings requested at certain times

⚑ MOFFAT CCC SITE
Hammerlands DG10 9QL 01683 220436
www.campingandcaravanningclub.co.uk
Open all year

Note: Lots of accommodation on the Old Carlisle Road (your route in), the High Street and Beechgrove

i Moffat Woollen Mill DG10 9EG
(leaflet point only) visitmoffat.co.uk

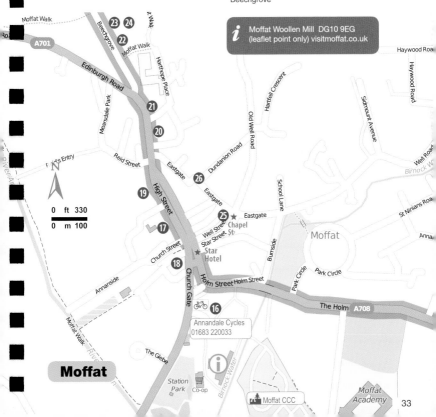

Imposing Caerlaverock Castle is one of the main tourist attractions in the area

Annan ~ Moffat (via Dumfries)

From Annan you head along NCN 7, briefly following a tranquil traffic free path alongside the river Annan before heading onto quiet roads. Drop down to the lovely village of Powfoot where great views open up over the Solway Firth. Heading inland you follow more quiet lanes, through tiny Ruthwell with its unusual Savings Bank Museum. Glide down towards the estuary with the opportunity to visit Caerlaverock National Nature Reserve or the well-preserved castle there. The run in to the interesting and picturesque market town of Dumfries follows the narrowing Nith estuary, past the tiny port of Kingholm Quay where you join a fine traffic free path. Soon after tranquil Dock Park you reach the historic centre. There is a lovely gentle road climb through rolling scenery to tiny Ae village before a truly testing section on rougher tracks through the Forest of Ae.

Route Info

Distance 84 km (52 miles)

Off road 28 km (17.5 miles)   Nice quality tarmac greets you on the short section out of Annan and on your entry to and exit from Dumfries. However, be aware the section through the Forest of Ae can be very rocky in places; real mountain bike territory, so the least you need is a bike with wide tyres and even then you'll have to push over the occasional rough, rocky section.

Terrain   You are lulled into a false sense of security by the easy ride around the Solway and Nith estuaries. A steady and pleasant road climb to Ae heralds a much harder series of off road climbs through the Forest of Ae which, as it's combined with some rough surfaces, is only for the fit and experienced used to riding in the wilds.

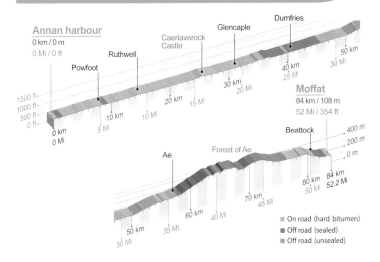

Annan harbour
0 km / 0 m
0 Mi / 0 ft

Powfoot

Ruthwell

Caerlaverock Castle

Glencaple

Dumfries

40 km / 25 Mi

50 km / 30 Mi

1500 ft - 1000 ft - 500 ft - 0 ft -

0 km / 0 Mi

5 Mi

10 km / 10 Mi

20 km / 15 Mi

30 km / 20 Mi

Moffat
84 km / 108 m
52 Mi / 354 ft

Beattock

Ae

Forest of Ae

400 m
200 m
0 m

50 km / 30 Mi

60 km / 40 Mi

70 km / 45 Mi

80 km / 50 Mi

84 km / 52.2 Mi

35 Mi

■ On road (hard bitumen)
■ Off road (sealed)
■ Off road (unsealed)

What to See & Do

For Annan and Moffat see previous chapter

• After dropping down to the coast at **Powfoot** a great expanse of beach and salt marsh accompanies you, with the Lake District rising in the distance behind the Solway Firth. The small, pretty village was originally a sea bathing resort but golf is more the favoured activity here nowadays. At tiny **Ruthwell** look out for the Savings Bank Museum and the remarkable Anglo-Saxon cross in the local church with both Latin and runic inscriptions.

• **Caerlaverock** is both a striking and very popular ruined castle and one of the most remarkable bird reserves in Britain.

The castle is an unusual triangular shape sitting in a picturesque moat and is crammed full of different architectural styles, reflecting its history between the 13th and 17th centuries, as it passed between the

Scots and the English several times. Nowadays a picturesque route break with cafe and admission fee!

The nearby nature reserve is best known for the huge numbers of Svalbard Barnacle geese that overwinter here, coming 2,000 miles from the Arctic where their summer home has become inhospitably cold.

• Turning up the **Nith Estuary** you pass through the former satellite harbour for Dumfries, **Glencaple**, now home to a permanently moored trawler used as a home. It's a lovely tranquil lookout over the estuary, with the days of fishing and boatbuilding long gone.

The entrance into Dumfries along the upper reaches of the estuary is classic Sustrans traffic free path, using high quality tarmac path from **Kingholm Quay** by the relaxing Swan pub. Then along the river to the picturesque green expanse of Dock Park.

Huge estuary views at Powfoot

Robert Burns statue,
Dumfries

• Robert Burns (see pg 18 for more detail) is everywhere in **Dumfries**, from the Robert Burns centre by the lovely river Nith, to the impressive town centre statue of him. Dumfries is much more than this though; there is a 15th century bridge (with a museum built into it), another museum with camera obscura, a fine fountain in the heart of the shopping area, Scotland's oldest working theatre and many other fine buildings.

The town was labelled Queen of the South by local poet David Dunbar, and the often crumbling facades of many fine buildings mean you can see why this might once have been the case. There is still much grandeur in the buildings here though. Most notably Greyfriars church is now well looked after and a great backdrop for the Burns statue. The historic facade of the County Hotel on the High Street has been retained and it remains

famous as The Young Pretender (Bonnie Prince Charlie) briefly had his headquarters here in1745, his kilted Jacobite rebel army camping in a field nearby.

The area around the train station boasts some very grand hotels. The town is also a hub for several National Cycle Network routes and has a good network of traffic free paths, and your route follows one of the best sections, alongside the River Nith and over Queen of the South Viaduct and onto the Maxwelltown Railway cyclepath as you head north out of town.

• The **Forest of Ae** centre has a handy mountain bike shop and cafe, possibly good preparation for the tough climb on forest tracks. You also pass through part of the rather surreal Harestanes Windfarm, the turbines reaching 126m in height. Extra mountain bike tracks were created as part of the project.

Accommodation

1 POWFOOT GOLF HOTEL

Links Avenue Powfoot DG12 5PN
01461 700254 thepowfootgolfhotel.com

2 SOLWAY SPORTING BREAKS

2 Queensberry Terrace Cummertrees DG12 5QF
01461 700333 solwaysportingbreaks.co.uk

BROOM FISHERIES CAMPSITE
Broom Farm Estate Newbie DG12 5PF
01461 700386 07749 426980
broom.broomfisheries.co.uk

QUEENSBERRY BAY HOLIDAY PARK
Powfoot DG12 5PN
01461 700205 queensberrybay.co.uk
Open January to November. Shoreside pitches
available

WEST MOSS-SIDE CCC CAMPSITE
Cummertrees DG12 5PU
01461 700485
campingandcaravanningclub.co.uk
CCC members only. Open all year.

For Annan town map and
accommodation see pgs 20-22

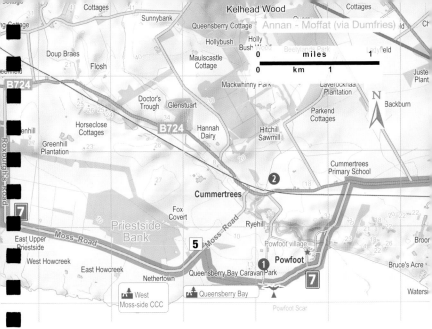

Directions

1 Follow route directions out of Annan to find yourself on Port Street (see town map pgs 20-22). Turn down Riverside Walk, following NCN 7 signs, to cross the lovely traffic free bridge **2**. Bend right under the bridge and pick up the path with the river Annan on your left (milepost just under bridge). Bear right onto a road to come to a junction by a factory and bear right onto Three Trees Road **3**.

4 Turn left onto the B724 then first left signed Powfoot to descend through this lovely estuaryside village. Follow the road through Queensberry Bay Caravan Park, still well signed as NCN 7 to rejoin a minor road at the other side of the site. Head left at the T-junction just out of the site **5**, picking up a very quiet road.

Attractive Powfoot

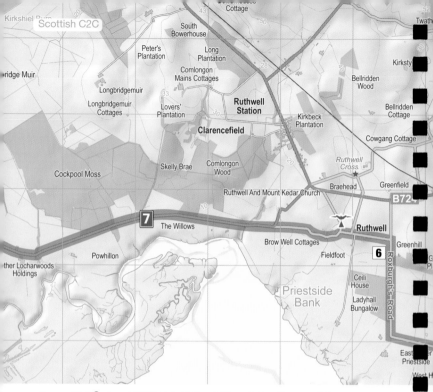

Turn next left **6**, signed NCN 7, into Ruthwell. Through the village turn left at the next T-junction. Head past Brow Well, a small spring visited by Robert Burns.
Climb to a T-junction in Bankend **7** and head left signed for Caerlaverock and Glencaple. Through the hamlet of Shearington there are turnings down to the left **8** if you wish to explore the Wildfowl and Wetland Trust site before you arrive at the entrance to the impressive Caerlaverock Castle.

Dumfries station is on a main north-south line linking Glasgow and Carlisle and so is serviced by **Scotrail**. Bike carriage is subject to space and, in some cases, to a cycle reservation. Reservations can be made by contacting 0330 303 0111.
You'll also come on this line if arriving from Stranraer, heading north all the way to Kilmarnock and changing to come back down on the Dumfries-Annan-Carlisle line, a journey of some 3 to 4+ hours. These are also **Scotrail** services.

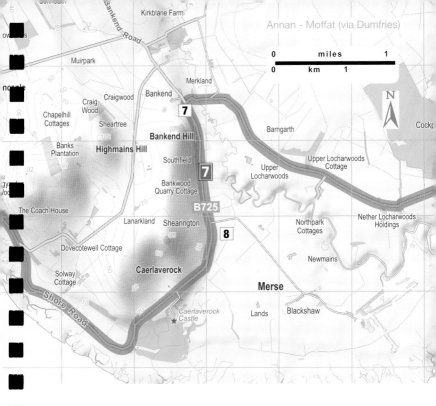

Annan - Moffat (via Dumfries)

NCN signing on the Nith Estuary

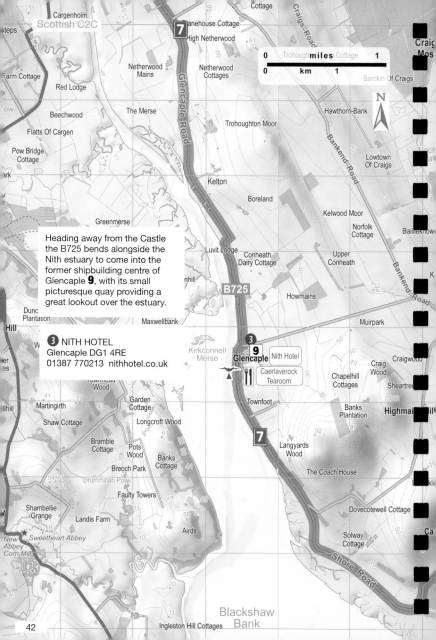

Heading away from the Castle the B725 bends alongside the Nith estuary to come into the former shipbuilding centre of Glencaple **9**, with its small picturesque quay providing a great lookout over the estuary.

3 NITH HOTEL
Glencaple DG1 4RE
01387 770213 nithhotel.co.uk

B725

3
9 Glencaple   Nith Hotel

Caerlaverock Tearoom

Climbing towards Dumfries you meet a roundabout **10** and head left, signed Kingholm Quay, initially on shared use pavement cycle lane, to descend and turn a corner to come to the picturesque little quay by the Swan pub. This lovely path hugs the river and you ignore the first traffic free bridge signed to Troqueer to bear left into the lovely Dock Park **11** on your approach to Dumfries centre.

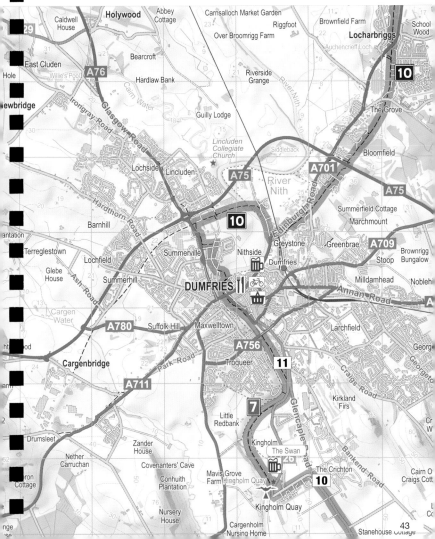

Out of Dock Park pass a series of four bridges, passing the Robert Burns centre on the opposite bank, before following NCN7 signs over a traffic free bridge **12** and straight on, onto College Street. Just past Goldie Avenue turn left onto the path round the edge of a small park.

Head over a roundabout and almost straightaway look for a right onto a path signed Maxwelltown Railpath **13**. Head right at the next junction – left is signed to several destinations including Kircudbright but you head right, unsigned, and follow this excellent straight path over the lovely Queen of the South viaduct and its monument to Kirkpatrick Macmillan.

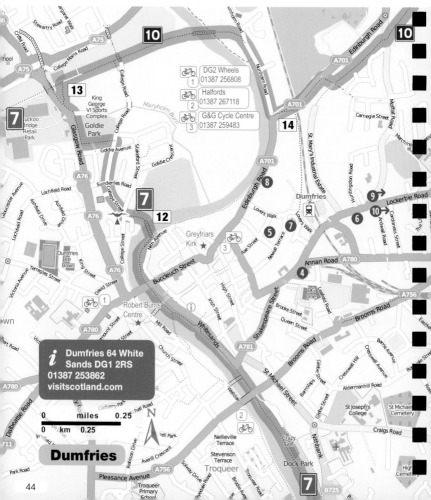

1 DG2 Wheels 01387 256808
2 Halfords 01387 267118
3 G&G Cycle Centre 01387 259483

Dumfries 64 White Sands DG1 2RS
01387 253862
visitscotland.com

0 — miles — 0.25
0 — km — 0.25

Dumfries

Meet a road and turn right, now firmly on Regional Route 10 signed in blue and white. At the busier Edinburgh Road bear left onto the pavement cycleway opposite, picking up signs for the Caledonian Cycleway **14**. Shortly jink right then left onto a leafy traffic free path, signed Bloomfield and Locharbriggs.

4 CAIRNDALE HOTEL
English Street DG1 2DF
01387 254111
cairndalehotel.co.uk

5 LINDEAN GUEST HOUSE
50 Rae Street DG1 1JE
01387 251888 07740 510452
lindeanguesthouse.co.uk

6 HUNTINGDON HOUSE HOTEL
18 St Mary's Street DG1 1LZ
01387 254893 huntingdonhotel.co.uk

7 FERINTOSH GUEST HOUSE
30, Lovers Walk DG1 1LX
01387 252262 ferintosh.net

8 LANGLANDS
8 Edinburgh Road DG1 1JQ
01387 266549 langlandsdumfries.co.uk

9 SAUGHTREE GUEST HOUSE
79 Annan Road DG1 3EG
01387 252358

10 THE PARK HOTEL
208 Annan Road DG1 3HE
01387 253840 dumfrieshotel.co.uk

Also lots of accommodation around the train station and along Annan Road

River Nith at Dumfries

The path ends at a road where you head left **15**, signed Beattock and Moffat (routes 10 and NCN 74, the latter actually meaning heading towards NCN74). The road climbs into the hills north of Dumfries with a smattering of route 10 signs; navigation however is easy, just ignore any minor turnings and go straight across any crossroads. Approaching Ae over open fells you see the conifer-covered mound of the forest of Ae ahead.

An easy start through the Forest of Ae, but be warned, the track becomes much more challenging

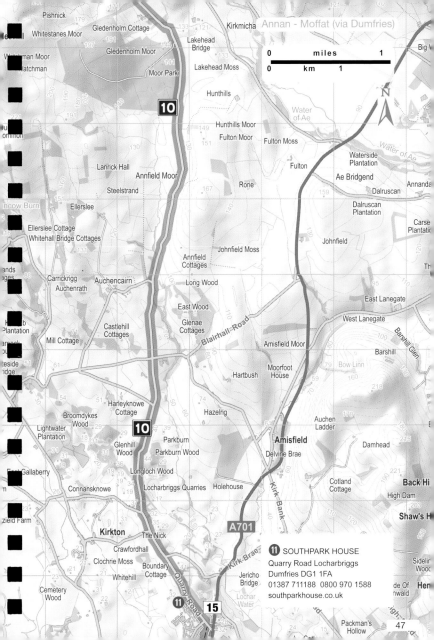

miles
1

km
1

10

10

A701

⑪ SOUTHPARK HOUSE
Quarry Road Locharbriggs
Dumfries DG1 1FA
01387 711188 0800 970 1588
southparkhouse.co.uk

⑪

15

47

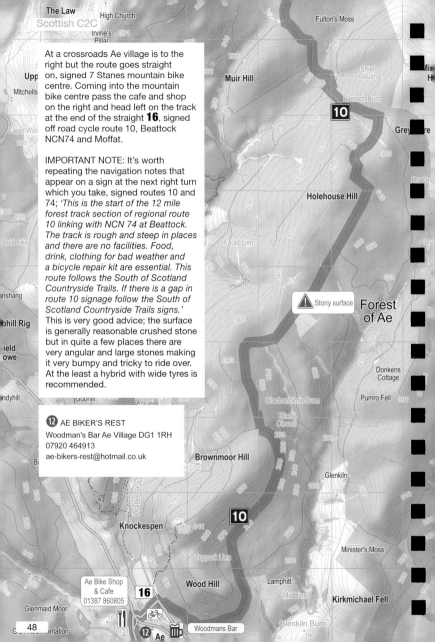

At a crossroads Ae village is to the right but the route goes straight on, signed 7 Stanes mountain bike centre. Coming into the mountain bike centre pass the cafe and shop on the right and head left on the track at the end of the straight **16**, signed off road cycle route 10, Beattock NCN74 and Moffat.

IMPORTANT NOTE: It's worth repeating the navigation notes that appear on a sign at the next right turn which you take, signed routes 10 and 74; *'This is the start of the 12 mile forest track section of regional route 10 linking with NCN 74 at Beattock. The track is rough and steep in places and there are no facilities. Food, drink, clothing for bad weather and a bicycle repair kit are essential. This route follows the South of Scotland Countryside Trails. If there is a gap in route 10 signage follow the South of Scotland Countryside Trails signs.'* This is very good advice; the surface is generally reasonable crushed stone but in quite a few places there are very angular and large stones making it very bumpy and tricky to ride over. At the least a hybrid with wide tyres is recommended.

12 AE BIKER'S REST
Woodman's Bar Ae Village DG1 1RH
07920 464913
ae-bikers-rest@hotmail.co.uk

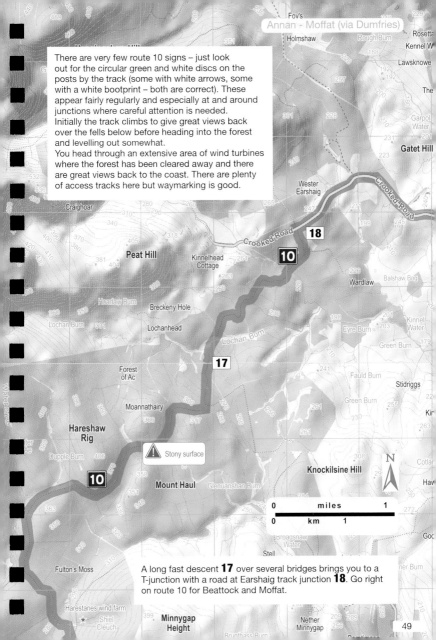

There are very few route 10 signs – just look out for the circular green and white discs on the posts by the track (some with white arrows, some with a white bootprint – both are correct). These appear fairly regularly and especially at and around junctions where careful attention is needed.

Initially the track climbs to give great views back over the fells below before heading into the forest and levelling out somewhat.

You head through an extensive area of wind turbines where the forest has been cleared away and there are great views back to the coast. There are plenty of access tracks here but waymarking is good.

⚠ Stony surface

miles 1

km 1

A long fast descent **17** over several bridges brings you to a T-junction with a road at Earshaig track junction **18**. Go right on route 10 for Beattock and Moffat.

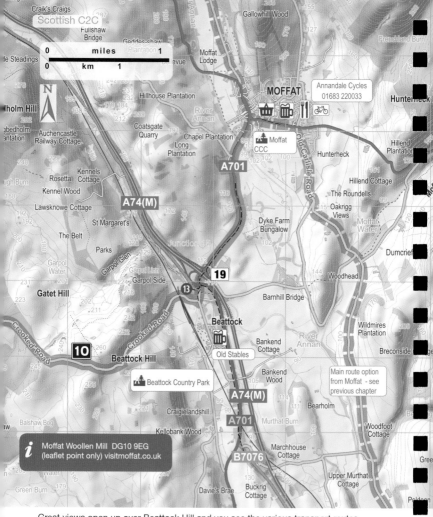

Great views open up over Beattock Hill and you see the various transport routes running along the valley beneath you. Over the small railway bridge hit a T-junction and go left to a roundabout by the A74(M). Use the pavement cycle lanes to pass under the A74M **19** to another roundabout then pick up the pavement cycle lane alongside the A701 towards Moffat. This spills you onto the road as you come into town then heads up the colourful and attractive main street.

BEATTOCK COUNTRY PARK
Beattock DG10 9RE
01683 300591 www.beattockcountrypark.com

13 LOCHHOUSE FARM
Beattock DG10 9SG
01683 300451 lochhousefarm.com
Secure storage & cyclists welcome

For Moffat town map and
accommodation see pg 33

The wonderfully quiet Crooked Road, west of Beattock

*The Devil's Beef Tub near
the route's highest point*

Moffat ~ Peebles

From Moffat you can choose either the off road option via Ericstane or the A701, both of which will bring you to the spectacular 'hollow in the hills' known as the Devil's Beef Tub, marking your approach to the highest point on the route at around 413m (1355ft). From here it's a wonderful sweeping descent down the Tweed Valley, with the landscape changing from the rather desolate feeling forestry plantations and wind farms higher up, to gentler pastures, backed by lovely rounded hills, downstream.

The Tweed is arguably at its finest around Peebles and at Lyne Station you may soon be able to choose to approach on the old railway (look out for evidence of this as you descend the Tweed Valley) which gives entry to Peebles over a magnificent viaduct and through a tunnel, or use a quiet road option which gives sweeping views of Cademuir Hill. Signing was absent at time of writing around Peebles, itself a handsome border town with lovely buildings and interesting shops.

Route Info

Distance 59.5 km (37 miles) Using the longer minor road route between Lyne Station and Peebles adds some 3.5km (2.2 miles)

Off road The main off road section is a 1.5km (0.9 mile) climb up an often rocky and steep farm track (rideable on a hybrid or mountain bike with wide tyres if you are pretty fit) out of Ericstane to the A701. The A701 out of Moffat provides a road alternative. A 4.5km (2.8 mile) section of railpath may in future take you from Lyne Station to Peebles. A very short off road section after Lyne Station crosses the Tweed.

Terrain A fairly tough ascent followed by a long sweeping descent. A gentle ride up the Old Edinburgh Road out of Moffat brings you to the hardest section of the main route, the off road climb up from Ericstane. There is a much more gradual road alternative using the A701 out of Moffat but you will have to mix in with some traffic and possibly timber lorries (though this is far from a busy road by 'A' road standards). After great views back down Annandale glide down the Tweed Valley. Heading towards Peebles a fine road route takes you around the beauty spot of Manor Sware with only moderate gradients whilst the possible future railpath option promises an even easier route end and a trip over a fine viaduct and through Neidpath tunnel.

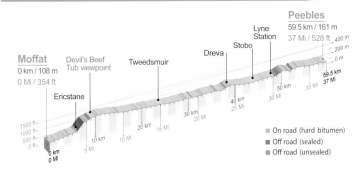

Moffat
0 km / 108 m
0 Mi / 354 ft

Ericstane

Devil's Beef Tub viewpoint

Tweedsmuir

Dreva

Stobo

Lyne Station

Peebles
59.5 km / 161 m
37 Mi / 528 ft

■ On road (hard bitumen)
■ Off road (sealed)
■ Off road (unsealed)

What to See & Do

• The climb up to the 150m deep hollow known as the **Devil's Beef Tub** is dramatic in itself with great views back down Annandale.

The Beef Tub is named after the Johnstone Clan, known as devils by their enemies, who hid pilfered cattle on the tub's steep sides.

It is also known as **Macleran's Loup** after a Jacobite who escaped capture by rolling down it!

Today the Annandale Way walking route traces a dramatic line around its top and the Borders Forest Trust protects the flora and fauna of much of the area, encouraging native species such as Black Grouse and Peregrine Falcon.

• Cresting the hill just past the Beef Tub you see a **memorial monument** on the right to two postmen of the Dumfries - Edinburgh mail who perished in a snowstorm in 1831 'after carrying the bags thus far'.

• Once past the Beef Tub the **Tweed Valley** accompanies you all the way into Peebles. One curious feature you might spot on the hillsides is the ringed stone wall enclosures known as stells. These date from before the current field pattern and were designed to shelter sheep from snow. The route into Peebles gives extensive views over Tweeddale with its gently curling river backed by forests of beech and Scots Pine, displaying a marvellous patchwork of intense colour in autumn.

The area is synonymous with **cycling**, both mountain biking at the nearby 7 Stanes centres of Glentress and Innerleithen and road cycling. May sees the two week long cycling festival known as TweedLove.

• Just off the route is **Broughton**, with handy teashop and a fine brewery, **Broughton Ales**.

View over the Tweed Valley from Peebles

Once busy, now deserted - the old Edinburgh road out of Moffat

• The **Upper Tweed Railway Paths** group is putting together funding and technical expertise to reopen the former line west of Peebles to cyclists and walkers all the way up to Tweedsmuir; negotiations were ongoing at the time of writing. When open the line will also give easy access to the tremendous viewpoint of **Manor Sware** near where you can see many of the elements that make up Tweeddale; not only the river and hills but the remains of the railway along the valley floor and a local quarry, source of greywacke stone used on many local buildings.

• **Dawyck Botanic Garden** is about 1km back up the B712 from where it is joined by the Dreva Road. Three hundred year old redwoods are housed in the fine arboretum.

• **Peebles** blends a handsome main street with glorious Tweed scenery. Attractions include the Old Parish Church at the western end of High Street, the handsome and popular Bridge Inn and the Tweeddale Museum and Gallery where there is also the John Buchan story. Buchan was a novelist, historian, journalist, politician and soldier. The novel *The Thirty Nine Steps* and being Governor General of Canada are amongst his many achievements! Those born here are *Gutterbluids* (old Scots for a low born person) but residents born elsewhere are known as *Stooriefoots*.

Scottish C2C

5

Annanhead Moss

Corehead Farm

The Skirtle
Dick's Hole
Cocklaw
Howes

miles

km

N

Acre Burn

Hill Cottage

Auldhousehill Bridge

⚠ Rough surface

Ericstane

4

3

Greenhill Dod

Auldhousehill Moss

Lane En—

Greenhillstairs

Archie's Hill

March Burn

Auchenrat Burn

2

Russell's Brae   Mountainblow   Fence Brae

Granton Farm

Shiel Burn

B719

A701

Blaemires Moss

Wee Hartfell

Grey Gill

Bassies' Brae

Meikleholmside Farm Cottage

Cross Burn

Meg's Hole

Archbank Belt

The Snout

Hind Hill

Hell's Hole

A74(M)

Road alternative to Ericstane off road option

A701

Reddings Farm

Blaebeck

Hind Gill   Moffat Well

B7076

Archbank Cottage

Middlegill Bridge

Craik's Craigs Plantation

Gallowhill Wood

Ritchie's Bushes

Fullshaw Bridge

Geddes-shaw Plantation

River Annan

Riverside Steadings

Bellevue

Moffat Lodge

Hillhouse Plantation

1

MOFFAT

🍴
🚲
🛒
🍺

River Annan

i visitsouthernscotland.co.uk
bestoftheborders.co.uk

oatsgate Quarry

Chapel Plantation

Long Plantation

Hunterheck

Plantation

Railway Cottage

y's

56

A701

Directions

1 Head out of Moffat up the High Street past the Stag Hotel and at the mini roundabout turn right up Beechgrove for the off road option. For the road option see * Alternative on road route out of Moffat below

! 🚲 Hybrid with wide tyres or mountain bike recommended for off road option.

Follow the lovely Old Edinburgh Road and pass over the little bridge **2** at Auchencat Burn. After 5.6km (3.5 miles) on this quiet road come to the farm at Ericstane **3** where you bear right by a small stone bridge on the left and just round the corner cross the wooden bridge by the ford. As you head across the farmyard look for the stony track over to the left by the trees - don't continue round the right hand bend towards the brick house.

The track ascends out of Ericstane and is very steep and quite rocky in places but the middle section is easier in terms of gradient and surface. At the track T-junction **4** turn right and climb up to the A701 and turn right onto it.

Gradually climb on the A701 with great views down Annandale, past the Covenanter Memorial **5** (easy to miss and a tricky road crossing if you want a look).

*Alternative on road route out of Moffat

If you want to avoid the steep and rocky off road section then don't turn right at this mini-roundabout on the edge of Moffat - bear left and simply follow the A701 out of town as it climbs gradually all the way to the point where the off road option joins on the right (signed as the Annandale Way).

The off road climb from Ericstane to the A701 and Devil's Beef Tub

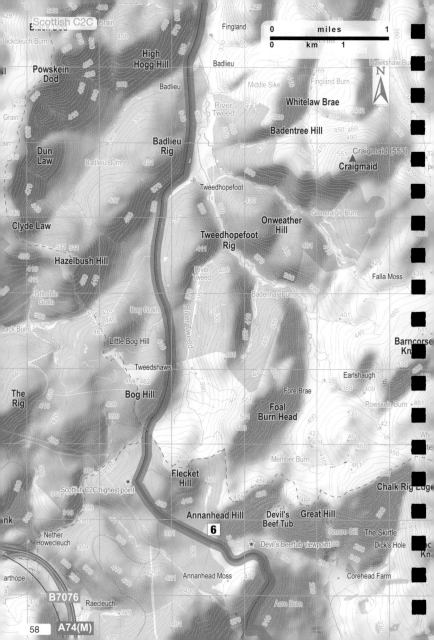

Continuing on the A701 pass the parking area **6** which gives a great view of Devil's Beef Tub with explanatory plaque about Robert the Bruce and his exploits near here. The A701 descends gradually, passing into the Scottish Borders area and past the source of the Tweed, through forestry plantation country.

Upper Tweeddale

Pass the Crook Inn **7**, unoccupied at the time of writing but with grand renovation plans. The views open out magnificently as you pass Stanhope **8** on the far side of the valley.

No rail stations en route, the nearest being Carstairs (24 km / 15 miles) which has onward connections to Glasgow taking 45 mins to 1 hour, and Lockerbie (minimum 25 km / 15.5 miles depending which route you cycle) which is the only station between Carlisle and Carstairs on that line.

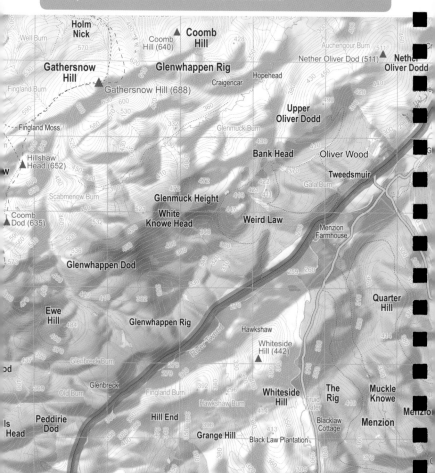

Accommodation

1 HEARTHSTANES COTTAGES
Near Tweedsmuir ML12 6QN
01899 225119
hearthstanes.com
Self catering cottages

2 CROOK INN
Community restoration project at the time of writing (i.e. not open) but watch this space (and check out their facebook page for the latest news).

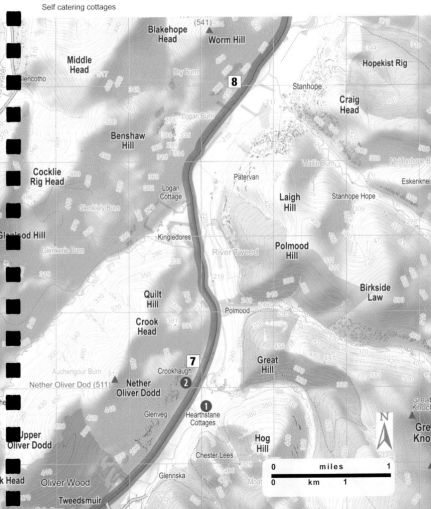

Some 27.5km (17 miles) after joining the A701 turn right **9** onto the B712 to Peebles. After about 1km (0.6 miles) on the B712 turn first left **10**, descending the minor road over a river and under an old railway bridge. At a T-junction turn right with magnificent views along the Tweed Valley. Descend back to the B712 and turn left onto it **11**. This long straight road carries some fast traffic so beware. It takes you past the entrance to Stobo Castle (private) **12**. Pass Stobo Castle entrance and turn next right **13** signed Lyne Station and Tor View B & B.

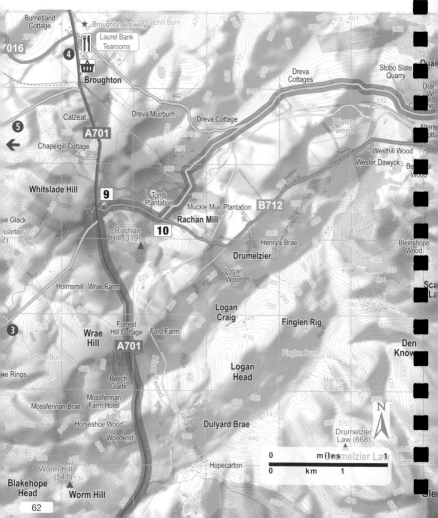

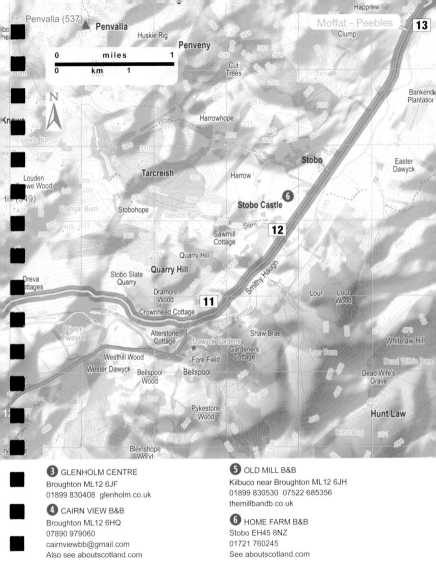

3 GLENHOLM CENTRE
Broughton ML12 6JF
01899 830408 glenholm.co.uk

4 CAIRN VIEW B&B
Broughton ML12 6HQ
07890 979060
cairnviewbb@gmail.com
Also see aboutscotland.com

5 OLD MILL B&B
Kilbuco near Broughton ML12 6JH
01899 830530 07522 685356
themillbandb.co.uk

6 HOME FARM B&B
Stobo EH45 8NZ
01721 760245
See aboutscotland.com

After passing Torview take the next right **14**, signed as a dead end.

Possible future route - Off road from Lyne Station - subject to landowner agreement.
The old railway viaduct here is where a fine traffic free route into Peebles may start
in future. It may follow the valley and cross a very elegant Victorian viaduct before
heading through a tunnel and entering the heart of Peebles (road alternative over
Old Manor Bridge should avoid the unlit tunnel).

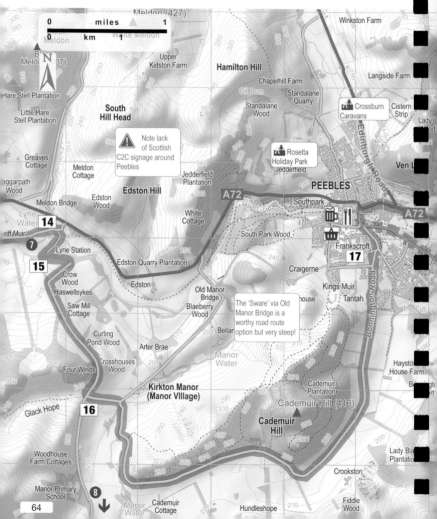

Current on road route from Lyne Station

Head through the hamlet of Lyne Station to the footbridge over the Tweed **15** and cross it to bend left onto the off road path through the trees. This emerges by a couple of cottages on your left; ignore the track that goes straight on through the gateposts and bend 90 degrees right onto tarmac. At the next T-junction turn left signed for Peebles **16** then shortly turn next right signed for Peebles via Cademuir.

Over tiny Manor Water you are soon on a tiny country road with glorious panoramas of the hills. After 3.5km / 2 miles a private road from Hundleshope joins from the right and a further 3 km / 2 miles on you come into Peebles' outskirts and soon pass the High School **17**, following Bonnington Road. Go right then left in quick succession at a pair of T-junctions to follow Springhill Road past Victoria Park. At the T-junction turn left over the bridge, taking you into the town centre.

7 TORVIEW HOUSE
Lyne Station nr Peebles EH45 8NP
01721 740255 torviewhouse.co.uk

8 CASTLEHILL KNOWE B&B
Kirkton Manor EH45 9JN
01721 740218 castlehill-knowe.co.uk

ROSETTA HOLIDAY PARK
Rosetta Road EH45 8PG
01721 720770
rosettaholidaypark.com
Open March to October

CROSSBURN CARAVANS
Edinburgh Road EH45 8ED
01721 720501
crossburn-caravans.com
Open Easter to October Tent sites and lodges

Self catering with a minimum 2 night stay is available a couple of kilometres or so north of Peebles at Winkston Farm, Edinburgh Road 01721 721264 winkstonholidays.co.uk and also in Peebles through Innerleithen Holiday Lets on 01896 830244 or 07963 930585

The Old Parish Church in Peebles

Peebles Accommodation

9 LINDORES GUEST HOUSE
60, Old Town EH45 8JE
01721 729040 lindoresgh.co.uk
Secure cycle storage

10 NEIDPATH INN
27–29, Old Town EH45 8JF
01721 724306 neidpathinn.co.uk

11 CROWN HOTEL
54, High Street EH45 8SW
01721 720239 crownhotelpeebles.co.uk

12 THE TONTINE HOTEL
High Street EH45 8AJ
01721 720892 tontinehotel.com

13 THE CROSS KEYS HOTEL
24, Northgate EH45 8RS
01721 723467 jdwetherspoon.co.uk

14 ROWANBRAE HOUSE
103, Northgate EH45 8BU
01721 721630
john@rowanbrae.freeserve.co.uk
Also see aboutscotland.com

15 THE GREEN TREE HOTEL
41, Eastgate EH45 8AD
01721 720582 greentreehotel.com

16 THE PARK HOTEL
Innerleithen Road EH45 8BA
01764 651550 parkpeebles.co.uk

17 WHITESTONE HOUSE B&B
69, High Street EH45 8BD
01721 720337
whitestonehouse70@gmail.com

18 KINGSMUIR HOUSE
Springhill Road EH45 9EP
01721 724413 kingsmuirhouse.co.uk

19 THE PEEBLES HYDRO
Innerleithen Road EH45 8LX
01764 651846 peebleshydro.co.uk

20 CRAIGUART
Eshiels, Innerleithen Road EH45 8LZ
01721 720219 craiguart.co.uk

Peebles High Street sculpture

Peebles

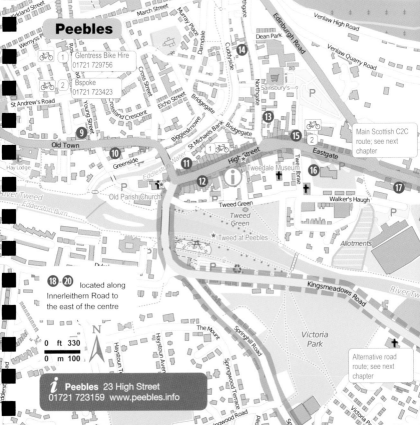

Peebles

1 Glentress Bike Hire
01721 729756

2 Bspoke
01721 723423

Main Scottish C2C
route; see next
chapter

18-20 located along
Innerleithern Road to
the east of the centre

0 ft 330
0 m 100

N

Alternative road
route; see next
chapter

i **Peebles** 23 High Street
01721 723159 www.peebles.info

67

Reaching the northern edge of the Moorfoot Hills reveals views towards Edinburgh and Arthur's Seat

Peebles - Dalkeith

This is a section of two distinct parts; the first sees you following the gentle meanders of the river Tweed between Peebles and Innerleithen and its varied and impressive landmarks, including grand Victorian spa hotels, fine bridges across the river and an attractive golf course. If you fancy some hills and more elevated views over the valley and a visit to Scotland's oldest inhabited house at Traquair (and don't mind mixing it with occasional traffic) then there is an alternative route, largely on the southern side of the valley.

After Innerleithen with its quirky history comes the steady but very long climb up a couple of valleys and across the moorland of the Moorfoot Hills to a wonderfully wide-ranging panorama across towards Edinburgh and the Pentland hills. A final gentle run alongside the River South Esk brings you to Dalkeith.

Route Info

Distance 51 km (31.5 miles) Taking the Peebles - Innerleithen road option adds about 6 km (4 miles).

Off road 10 km (6 miles) Mainly wonderful smooth tarmac along a former railway between Peebles and Innerleithen. A route diversion near Bonnyrigg, approaching Dalkeith, uses pavement cycle lane but is subject to change due to the new station being built there; this should be very well surfaced when complete.

Terrain
As you would expect the Peebles - Innerleithen railpath has only the gentlest of gradients whilst the on road alternative offers a couple of short but testing climbs. The climb over the Moorfoot hills features long and steady gradients that are generally not too testing unless you have a headwind when they become a serious challenge! It's largely downhill or on the flat coming into Dalkeith.

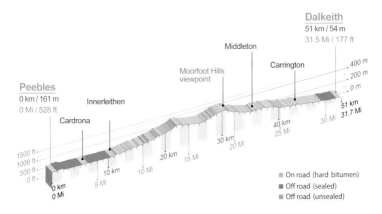

What to See & Do

• Spa therapy and hotels are very much in evidence on this section. The magnificent **Peebles Hydro** is an early 20th-century country house hotel and spa resort found right by the railpath to Innerleithen and one of two hydropathic hotels left in Scotland. Rebuilt in 1907, it served as a hospital for injured service personnel during WWII before reverting to hotel use.

St Ronan's Well at Innerleithen experienced its heyday before the sumptuous Peebles Hydro spa was built and you can still take the waters at St Ronan's, look around the museum or simply admire this beautiful little building and look across the valley to see the outline of the Iron Age Pirn Hill Fort. Founded in the 1820s, St Ronan's later expanded its activities to include bathing facilities and a bottling plant and many of Innerleithen's town traditions are derived from its existence.

• **7 Stanes Mountain Biking** is found at several forests in the area.

• **Golfing** is much in evidence on this section, with spectacularly located courses between Peebles and Innerleithen and in the valley bottom as you head up the Leithen Water and into the Moorfoot Hills.

• **Kailzie Gardens** are accessible from the alternative road route and as well as garden walks you can visit the tearooms / restaurant and the nature centre with live osprey cams.

Peebles Hydro

Descending the Moorfoots is easy on the eye and the legs

• The **Tweed Valley railpath** is a textbook example of how to convert an old railway into a splendid high quality traffic free ride along a wide strip of tarmac and includes a tunnel near the Peebles end and a bridge near Innerleithen. Peebles once had two railway stations where none exist today; the Caledonian Railway linked to Symington whilst the North British Railway ran from Edinburgh.

• Despite lacking the size, wealth and good looks of nearby Peebles, **Innerleithen** has plenty of interest for visitors. Pirn Hill Fort and St Ronan's Well (see opposite) are on the route out which also leads to the beautifully appointed town golf course.

On the Friday of the third week in July look out for the unique Cleikum Ceremony (part of the St Ronan's Games). Apparently St Ronan engaged the Devil in combat, the Cleikum Ceremony being a re-enactment play whereby a local boy plays the saint and drives the devil out of town.

• A classic climb wends its way gradually up through the **Moorfoot Hills** to a magnificent lookout over Edinburgh, the Firth of Forth and the Pentland Hills. Upland blanket bogs here support distinctive moorland plants and animals, including grouse, hares and cloudberries.

• The area around **Dalkeith** is most notable for its historic attractions of **Newbattle Abbey** and **Dalkeith Palace**. The former, once a Cistercian abbey and now a college and wedding venue, is surrounded by 125 acres of lovely parkland. The latter is en route as you leave Dalkeith and is covered in the next chapter on page 84.

Directions
Traffic free option

1 Head east along Peebles Main Street, the A72, and at the second eastern entrance to the Hydro hotel pick up cycle signs for Glentress, Cardrona and Innerleithen (NCN 1) and shortly up this tarmac track turn right **2** onto the excellent tarmac railpath. A lovely woodland section descends to the A72 and shortly passes under it. If you want to check out the exceedingly popular trails at Glentress Forest these are signed on a spur from the railpath **3**.

Road option

1 Cross to the south side of the main road bridge in Peebles and carry on on this road, the B7062, out of town. Pass Kailzie Gardens tearoom entrance **2a** and climb then drop down past Kailzie Bunk lodge.

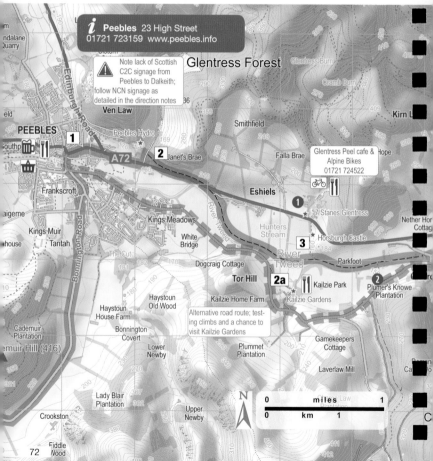

Peebles 23 High Street
01721 723159 www.peebles.info

Note lack of Scottish C2C signage from Peebles to Dalkeith; follow NCN signage as detailed in the direction notes

Glentress Forest

Glentress Peel cafe & Alpine Bikes
01721 724522

Alternative road route; testing climbs and a chance to visit Kailzie Gardens

GLENTRESS FOREST LODGES

Linnburn Farm, Eshiels EH45 8NA
07840 283 22 glentressforestlodges.co.uk
Luxury camping pod style accommodation with
heating and self-catering.

2 KAILZIE BUNKHOUSE

Kailzie EH45 9HT 01721 723334 bunk-house.co.uk
Opposite entrance & car park to Cardrona Forest.
Secure cycle storage
Part of Kailzie Gardens which also has a self
catering cottage
01721 720007 kailziegardens.com

No rail stations within easy cycling distance; Carstairs station is more than 45km / 28 miles west of Peebles along the Tweed Valley Cycle Route. It gives direct onward connections along the Ayr-Glasgow-Edinburgh line, with Edinburgh being around 30 mins and Glasgow 40 mins from Carstairs. Although Edinburgh is less than 40km / 25 miles cycling from Peebles in a direct line, this would involve riding the very busy, fast and dangerous A703 trunk road. From autumn 2015 there should be a station at Tweedbank near Galashiels on the new Borders Railway, some 23km / 14 miles along the Tweed Valley; an easy ride along existing cycle route. See bordersrailway.co.uk for more detail.

Glentress Forest Lodges

Follow the railpath across a golf course emerging in front of Cardrona village store **4** and crossing the roundabout onto Cardrona Way. Signs for Innerleithen Paths lead you through this pretty modern estate, taking you left down Leeburn View. Pick up the railpath again **5** across the golf course and recross the Tweed on a delightful new traffic free bridge. Continue on the railpath until it meets a road (Traquair Road) **6** in Innerleithen. Go left, passing the Traquair Arms Hotel to the main road. Head right down the Main Street looking out for the onward route shortly, on your left, following NCN 1 signs to Middleton and Bonnyrigg **7** (both route options have now joined on Leithen Road). Pass the war memorial; note Pirn Hill Fort and St Ronan's Well are just off the route here (see What to See & Do).

Road option continued

The road option passes Cardrona village down to the left **3a** (you can join the off road option here if you wish by turning left and right onto Cardrona Way). Pass the entrance to Traquair House and descend and climb to a T-junction **4a** by a stone cross heading left, signed Innerleithen on the B709. Turn right as the road bends left, signed Elibank, and immediately pass the car parking area for Elibank and Traquair Forest mountain bike trails which are on the opposite side of the road. As you descend look out for the old rail bridge across the Tweed down to the left and head off the road on a path that zig zags down the hill to it **5a**. Follow NCN1 signs as the path crosses the River Tweed on the lovely former railway bridge then bends right through housing to a road. Turn left off this path down Montgomery Street and at the end head straight on across a small metal bridge to come to another road and turn right. Continue up Leithen Crescent to the main road. The route continues straight on up Leithen Rd whilst the town centre is down to the left.

3 MACDONALD CARDRONA HOTEL
Cardrona EH45 8NE
0844 879 9024
macdonaldhotels.co.uk

4 TWEED VIEW B & B
7, Mains Farm Steading Cardrona EH45 9HL
01896 831771 tweedview.co.uk

5 CADDON VIEW
14 Pirn Road Innerleithen EH44 6HH
01896 830208 caddonview.co.uk

6 TRAQUAIR ARMS HOTEL & COTTAGES
Innerleithen EH44 6PD
01896 83229 traquairarmshotel.co.uk

7 CRUMBS B&B
25, St. Ronan's Terrace Innerleithen EH44 6RB
01896 833846 crumbsbakingbandb.co.uk

8 GLEDE KNOWE GUEST HOUSE
16, St. Ronan's Terrace Innerleithen EH44 6RB
01896 831295 gledeknowe.co.uk

St Ronan's Well

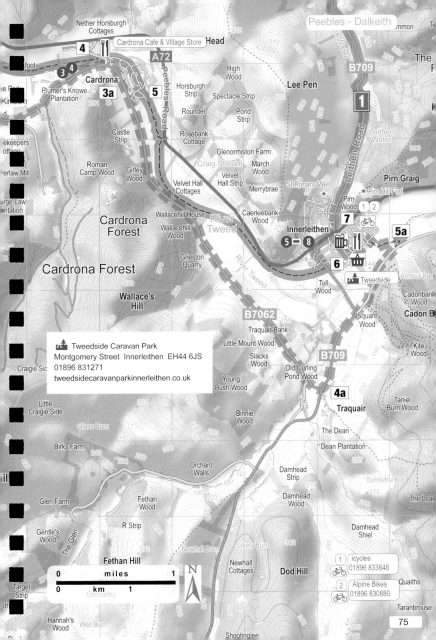

Nether Horsburgh Cottages

Cardrona Cafe & Village Store **Head**

4 🍴

A72

3 **4**

Cardrona

Plumer's Knowe Plantation

3a

5

High Wood

Horsburgh Strip

Spectacle Strip

Pond Strip

Roundel

Rosebank Cottage

B709

Lee Pen

502

Leithen Water

Castle Strip

Roman Camp Wood

Girley Wood

Glenormiston Farm

Craig Stream

March Wood

St Ronans Well

Leithen Road

Pirn Graig

Pirn Hill Fort

Velvet Hall Cottages

Velvet Hall Strip

Merrybrae

Pirn Wood

1 **2**

Cardrona Forest

Wallacehill House

Wallacehill Wood

River Tweed

Caerleebank Wood

Innerleithen

7 🚲

5a

Cardrona Forest

Grieston Quarry

River Tweed

5 🚂 **8**

🍺 🍴

6

🛒

Wallace's Hill

Toll Wood

Armour Burn

🏕 Tweedside

Cadonbank Wood

Cadon B

B7062

149

Square Wood

Craigie Side

🏕 Tweedside Caravan Park
Montgomery Street Innerleithen EH44 6JS
01896 831271
tweedsidecaravanparkinnerleithen.co.uk

Traquair Bank

Little Mount Wood

161

Slacks Wood

B709

Kite Wood

Young Bush Wood

153

Old Curling Pond Wood

202

4a

Little Craigie Side

Binnie Wood

Traquair

Taniel Burn Wood

Glass Burn

Birks Farm

Orchard Walls

191

The Dean

Dean Plantation

Damhead Strip

Dumbetha Bog

272

Glen Farm

Damhead Wood

The Lea

Fethan Wood

R Strip

Gentle's Wood

The Glen

Damhead Shiel

Fethan Hill

372

Newhall Burn

Likely Burn

342

280

221

Glenvalley

Newhall Cottages

Dod Hill

Quaiths

Target Strip

Hannah's Wood

Well Burn

Shootinglee

Taranbrouse

0   miles   1

0   km   1

N

🚲 **1** icycles
01896 833848

🚲 **2** Alpine Bikes
01896 830880

75

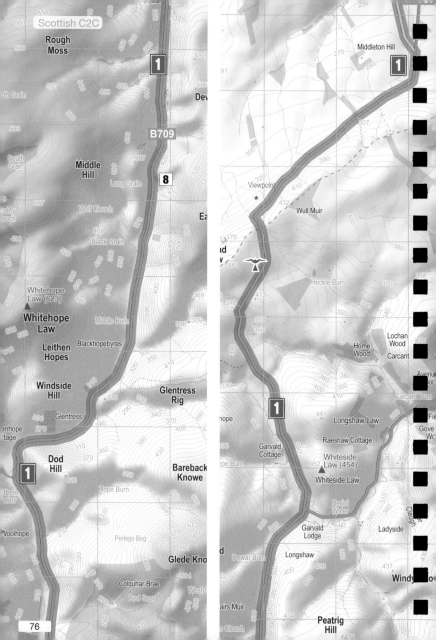

Rough Moss

1

Dev

B709

Middle Hill

8

Long Grain

Ea

Wolf Cleuch

Black Grain

Whitehope Law (623)

Whitehope Law

Middle Burn

Leithen Hopes

Blackhopebyres

Windside Hill

Glentress

Glentress Rig

nhope tage

Dod Hill

1

Bareback Knowe

Voolhope

Hope Burn

Perlego Bog

Glede Kno

Colquhar Brae

Red Scar

West

Middleton Hill

1

Viewpoint

Wull Muir

nd

Heckle Burn

Lochan Wood

Home Wood

Carcant

Aven

Carcant Burn

1

hope

Longshaw Law

Garvald Cottage

Raeshaw Cottage

Whiteside Law (454)

Whiteside Law

e Burn

Heriot Water

Garvald Lodge

Longshaw

Ladyside

Cleugh

Windy

Dewar Burn

Peatrig Hill

airs Cleuch

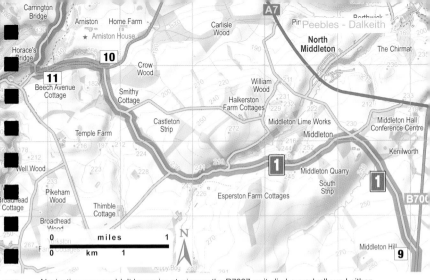

Navigation now couldn't be easier, staying on the B7007 as it climbs gradually up Leithen Water and then Glentress Water before cresting a watershed **8** and descending Dewar Burn. Swing left, passing the right turn down the B709 to Heriot. Another gradual climb takes you through a cutting and past the small windfarm. Great views over the Pentlands, Edinburgh and the Firth of Forth open out as you swing right to descend the Moorfoot Hills. After 3km / 1.8 miles of descent, turn left for Middleton **9**, still on NCN 1. At the next crossroads turn left, keeping on NCN 1 towards Bonnyrigg and Edinburgh. Simply remain on this lovely winding road, following NCN 1 signs, ignoring a minor left then a minor right at the hamlet of Castleton. About 4.5 km / 2.8 miles after Middleton meet the B6372 and turn left **10** for Temple and Penicuik.

Swing right over the impressive bridge across the river South Esk **11** (Temple to your left here) and immediately turn right, signed Carrington and NCN1. Climb away from the river and pass Carrington Mill.

Into the Moorfoot Hills

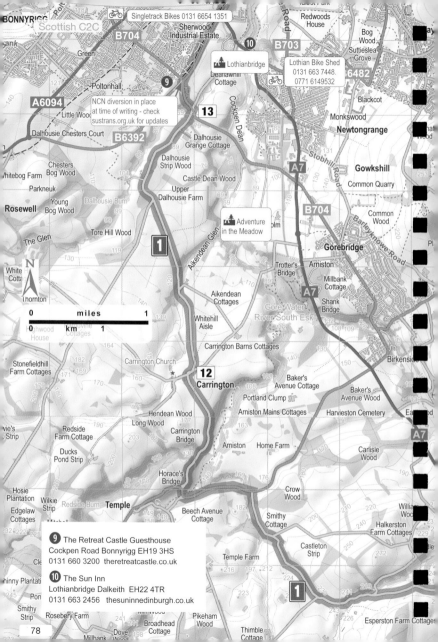

BONNYRIGG Scottish C2C

Singletrack Bikes 0131 6654 1351

B704

Sherwood Industrial Estate

Redwoods House

Bog Wood

Suttieslea Grove

Poltonhall

Green

10 Lothianbridge

Deanawhill Cottage

B703

Lothian Bike Shed 0131 663 7448. 0771 6149532

6482

9

A6094

Little Wood

NCN diversion in place at time of writing - check sustrans.org.uk for updates

13

Cockpen Dean

Blackcot

Monkswood

Newtongrange

Dalhousie Chesters Court

B6392

Dalhousie Grange Cottage

Chesters Bog Wood

Whitebog Farm

Parkneuk

Young Bog Wood

Dalhousie Strip Wood

Castle Dean Wood

Upper Dalhousie Farm

A7

Stobhill Road

Gowkshill

Common Quarry

Rosewell

Dalhousie Burn

Tore Hill Wood

B704

Common Wood

The Glen

Adventure in the Meadow

olm

Gorebridge

Barleyknowe Road

Pl

White Cotta

Aikendean Glen

Trotter's Bridge

Arniston

N

Thornton

Aikendean Cottages

Millbank Cottage

A7

Shank Bridge

miles   1

Whitehill Aisle

Gore Water River South Esk

Highwood House

km   1

Carrington Barns Cottages

Birkenside

Stonefieldhill Farm Cottages

Carrington Church

12
Carrington

Baker's Avenue Cottage

Baker's Avenue Wood

A7

Portland Clump

Arniston Mains Cottages

Harvieston Cemetery

vie's Strip

Hendean Wood

Long Wood

Carrington Bridge

Arniston

Home Farm

Carlisle Wood

Redside Farm Cottage

Ducks Pond Strip

Horace's Bridge

Crow Wood

Willia Wo

Hosie Plantation

Wilkie Strip

Redside Burn

Temple

Beech Avenue Cottage

Smithy Cottage

Halkerston Farm Cottages

Edgelaw Cottages

Castleton Strip

9 The Retreat Castle Guesthouse
Cockpen Road Bonnyrigg EH19 3HS
0131 660 3200 theretreatcastle.co.uk

Temple Farm

hinny Plantati

Pon

10 The Sun Inn
Lothianbridge Dalkeith EH22 4TR
0131 663 2456 thesuninnedinburgh.co.uk

1

Smithy Strip

Rosebery Farm

Dove Millbank

Broadhead Cottage

Pikeham Wood

Thimble Cottage

Esperston Farm Cottages

Come to a T-junction in Carrington **12**. The lovely 18th century church is to the left but you head right then immediate left for Cockpen and Dalkeith. Follow NCN1 signs, heading through Dalhousie to come to a crossroads with the B704 (church up to left). Turn left here **13** (caution fast road) and follow the road past the church to Cockpen Road Roundabout. Here you may have to follow temporary yellow and black NCN1 / 196 route signs which take you right onto the pavement cycle lane on the far side of the roundabout (the old NCN 1 route went straight on into Bonnyrigg to pick up the railpath - the new rail station at Dalkeith and the new line through the borders has meant rerouting).

Descend the cycle lane and head across Hardengreen roundabout staying on the pavement cycle lane alongside the B6392 for Eskbank and Hardengreen Industrial Estate.

ADVENTURE IN THE MEADOW

The Mansion of Kirkhill
Gorebridge EH23 4LJ
0131 240 0080 / 07833 085585
adventureinthemeadow.wordpress.com

LOTHIANBRIDGE CARAVAN PARK

Craigesk Newtongrange EH22 4TP
0131 663 6120

At Carrington

The cycle lane merges with the road and at the next roundabout **14** head right onto Eskbank Road CARE REQUIRED BUSY ROAD. Follow this all the way into Dalkeith, heading straight on at the next two junctions to come through the town centre to the entrance to Dalkeith Country Park. For your route choice here see the next chapter. The Scottish C2C goes straight on here whilst the link to NCN 1 heads right along Musselburgh Road out of Dalkeith.

NOTE: The route approaching Dalkeith was a temporary route introduced early 2015. For future route developments see sustrans.org.uk Ultimately there will be a new traffic free route here.

⑪ GLENARCH GUEST HOUSE
Melville Road Eskbank Dalkeith EH22 3NJ
0131 454 0985 glenarchhouse.co.uk

⑫ PREMIER INN
Melville Dykes Road Dalkeith EH18 1AN
0871 527 9290 premierinn.com

⑬ THE COUNTY HOTEL
152 – 156, High Street Dalkeith EH22 1AY
0131 663 3495 countyhoteldalkeith.co.uk

⑭ WESTER COWDEN FARMHOUSE
Wester Cowden Dalkeith EH22 2QA
0131 663 3052

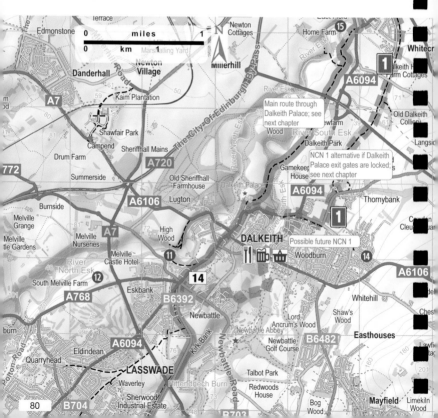

⑮ SMEATON HOUSE B&B
Salters Road Dalkeith EH22 2NJ
0131 669 0077

FUTURE ROUTE NOTE
Dashed line on map below shows possible
future alignment of NCN1 from Eskbank to
Woodburn after Dalkeith's new rail station is
open. For route updates see sustrans.org.uk

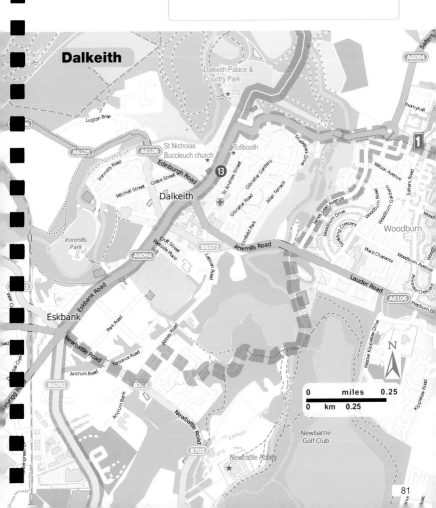

A wonderful finish to your route, the Forth Rail Bridge

Dalkeith ~ Forth Bridge

This wonderful end to the route combines easy cycling with a mix of impressive sights. From Dalkeith you pass through the country park on a beautiful estate road before picking up the traffic free River Esk path all the way to the coast at Musselburgh.

Magnificent promenade riding follows, notably at Musselburgh, Portobello and Silverknowes. Lovely little Cramond village and the following conservation area are havens of tranquility and refreshment away from the wilds of the Firth of Forth, as you skirt around and over the pretty River Almond.

The final section through the grounds of Dalmeny House is a wonderfully scenic and tranquil prelude to a symphonic finish as the route runs close by the coast, with magnificent views of the Firth of Forth bridge opening up in front of you. The masterpiece of Victorian engineering still has the world's second longest single cantilever span. The 'official' finish is right by the base of the bridge, just next to the amenities and attractions of pretty South Queensferry.

Route Info

Distance 37 km (23 miles)

Off road 8 km (5 miles)   Generally great quality tarmac or concrete. The track through Dalmeny estate is very variable, from smooth tarmac to occasional quite bumpy stone surfacing; a hybrid bike is recommended. There is a tarmac alternative from Cramond Brig Toll Bridge area to the route finish; quicker but overall less scenic.

Terrain Generally downhill, mostly easy traffic free riding.

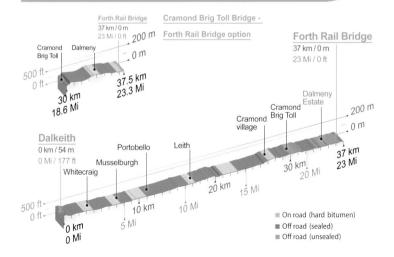

What to See & Do

• **Dalkeith Palace** and its magnificent parkland is encountered en route, just at the end of Dalkeith High Street. The upper end of the High Street has some handsome buildings, including the County Hotel, St Nicholas Buccleuch church, the quirky Tollbooth (former weighhouse, town court, prison and stagecoach post) and the old Corn Exchange.

• **Edinburgh centre**, although not on the route, is just a short ride away. For a centre route option (not signed as the Scottish C2C) see pages 106 and following.

• The route joins the coast at **Musselburgh**, after following the pretty river Esk here. If you take epithets literally you might feel comfortable leaving your bike unlocked here as Musselburgh is known as "The Honest Toun", and celebrates this by the annual election of the Honest Lad and Lass. It comes from the fact that a local aristocrat was cared for through illness by locals who declined any reward from his successor.

The town is also known for its golf links and racecourse.

• A fine promenade ride awaits through the traditional seaside resort **Portobello**, with its beautiful sweep of beach. 20th century decline has been replaced by 21st century renaissance, helped by improved seawater quality and strong community pride in the town's Victorian legacy, typified by the lovely Victorian baths, still open for bathing (Turkish baths and an aerotone - an early jacuzzi - also).

Meet the sea at Musselburgh.

Buying supplies on Portobello promenade

• Once a tough port, now rather more gentrified, **Leith** has something of the feeling of a Dutch or Belgian port, reflecting its historical links with the Northern European maritime trading organisation, the Hanseatic League. Today it is a popular and trendy eating and relaxing spot, a multicultural melting pot with plenty of sights and much to delight the palate. **Leith Links** are very scenic.

• Just a couple of minutes ride off the route, moored in the Port of Leith behind Ocean Terminal shopping centre, is the former **Royal Yacht Britannia**. With many original 1953 features, and preserved in every detail, largely as she was when decommissioned, in 1997, she travelled over one million miles on both state duties and royal holidays.

• Beyond Leith, **Granton** is suffering the effects of stalled redevelopment in a post industrial wasteland but the lighthouse building has a quirky history; it appears to be inland because it was never a true lighthouse, but once part of the Northern Lighthouse Stores and Buoy Yard. The 'lighthouse' used to test lighthouse light bulbs before they were shipped elsewhere.

• **Cramond** has a couple of very attractive spots, one by the coast as you turn inland, then another at the conservation area around the River Almond, crossed on a lovely ancient bridge. Cramond Island can be visited at low tide and the massive concrete bollards exposed then are the remains of an anti-submarine barrage.

85

• **Dalmeny Park** houses the magnificent buildings of Dalmeny House and the previous home of the Roseberry aristocrats, Barnbougle Castle. The route passes in front of the house, but access (including tearooms) is mid-summer only.

• Journey's end around **the Forth Bridges** is a suitably grand place to sit and reflect on your adventure, drinking in views of the 1890 Forth rail bridge and the later road bridge. The Forth Estuary holds fascinating sights too, not least its islands. **Inchmickery** Island can be seen at many points on your ride along the coast after Musselburgh, its battleship like silhouette showing how the WWII gun emplacements are still in remarkably good condition.

The even tinier island of **Inch Garvie** has been inhabited in the past but today its most important function is to help hold up part of the Forth Rail Bridge.

• Further afield and best known of all the Forth Islands is **Inchcolm**. Like Inchmickery it is fortified, but attracts visitors because it houses Scotland's most complete monastic house, a beautiful **Augustinian Abbey**. There are just two residents, wardens of Historic Scotland. There are currently two ferry services and one charter yacht company that operate trips to Inchcolm island, and allow passengers 1.5 hours to explore the island. The Maid of the Forth and the Forth Belle both operate from the Hawes Pier in South Queensferry between Easter and late October. Edinburgh Boat Charters (sailboats) operates year round from Port Edgar in South Queensferry. You also have the chance to spot dolphins, porpoises and perhaps even Minke whales.

Dalmeny House

Inchmickery Island

• Undoubtedly one of the UK's engineering wonders, the Forth Bridge, popularly known as the **Forth Rail Bridge** to distinguish it from the nearby road bridges, has to be one of the finest finishes to any cycle route anywhere.

Opened in 1890, this magnificent cantilever bridge was assessed by engineers in 2007 and the structure thought to be sound for at least another 100 years. Its key facts are just as impressive as your first sight of it; the 53,000 tonne structure rises 110m above the water at the top of the cantilevers and 200 trains daily still use it. The 2002 restoration programme lasted 10 years and the red paint used was especially mixed to match the original colour. It's perhaps equally astonishing that it got built in the first place as 1879 had seen the Tay Bridge disaster when a much less well-designed lattice work bridge further north at Dundee collapsed whilst a train was crossing, killing all on board.

• The Forth estuary's southern hinterland boasts the pretty village of **Dalmeny**, with cottages ranged around a green and an ancient church plus the attractive town of **South Queensferry**. Notable buildings include the Hawes Inn, almost under the Forth Bridge and a fine place to celebrate the end of your route (it features in Robert Louis Stevenson's novel Kidnapped) and the Tollbooth, with a clock-tower built in 1720.

• There is more great riding to be had on the National Cycle Network around the Forth; use the cycle lanes across the Forth Road Bridge to get a different perspective on the two behemoths from **North Queensferry**. Carry on north up NCN 1 through **Inverkeithing** then head west of NCN 764 to come to the heart of ancient Scotland and its first capital, **Dunfermline**.

What to See & Do - Edinburgh Option
(for route details see pg106 and following)

• You can choose to head off the main Scottish C2C and through **Edinburgh centre**.
On the ride in to the centre (starting between Musselburgh and Joppa) there are plenty of grassed areas ideal for a picnic stop.
• Short detours from the route will take you at the Joppa end around the parkland of the **Newhailes estate,** with its lovely neo-Palladian house or at the Edinburgh end to **Craigmillar Castle**, again parkland but this time with a well preserved medieval castle.
• Approaching the city the distinctive volcanic mass of **Arthur's Seat** heralds a welter of things to see.
• Leave the route just before the Innocent Railway Tunnel and head up to **Holyrood Park** for an exhilarating climb around Arthur's Seat and great views over the city.

A shared use path starting at the second roundabout after the entrance to the park follows the road round passing the Scottish Parliament and the Palace of Holyroodhouse.
• On the southern edge of the park **Duddingston village** has a loch which attracts a wide variety of birdlife, a beautiful terraced garden (**Dr. Neil's Garden**), a twelfth century church and the **Sheep Heid Inn**, thought to be Edinburgh's oldest pub.
• The **Innocent Railway tunnel** (the railway being so named because it was still horse drawn in an age which thought steam engines dangerous) comes before a bit of zigzagging through housing and city streets (variety of eating places here), leading to the wide expanses of the **The Meadows** parkland.

Innocent Railpath approaching Edinburgh

Middle Meadows Walk

• At the top of Middle Meadows Walk you enter the **UNESCO World Heritage Site** area and are heading for the Old Town which stretches from the mighty **medieval castle** high up on its rock to the **Palace of Holyroodhouse** and contains some of the city's best-loved icons.

• The first of these you see may be the statue of **Greyfriars Bobby,** situated at the corner of Candlemaker Row and George IV Bridge. This Skye Terrier allegedly spent 14 years guarding the grave of his master in nearby Greyfriars churchyard, where the dog himself was buried when he died in 1872.

• Off the route but worth a detour, **Grassmarket** is the historic market place of Edinburgh Old Town and one time place of executions. It has fine views of the castle.

• Crossing the **Royal Mile**, a name coined to cover the line of streets between the castle and Holyroodhouse, the route takes you down The Mound alongside the elegant **West Princes Street Gardens** and onto Princes Street itself, renowned for its shops and the **Scott Monument** in **East Princes Street Gardens.**

• **Princes Street** is the southernmost street of the New Town, which was constructed between 1767 and 1890 to ease overcrowding and discourage migration to London.

• Across Princes Street and at the top of the hill, **George Street** is the central street of the New Town. Wide, elegant and well furnished with a cocktail of cafes, statuary and double-barrelled, continental style cycle lanes, it extends from Charlotte Square at the western end, where Bute House is the official residence of the First Minister to St. Andrew Square, on the route at the eastern end from where Viscount Melville, an 18th century Home Secretary, surveys the scene from the top of his 150 foot high column.

• Wide cobbled streets lead you past graceful stone terraced buildings through the impressive Drummond Place to **King George V Park** where you pass through the Rodney Street railway tunnel to leave the city and head off towards Leith along the Warriston Path (diverting onto the main Scottish C2C along the Chancelot Path). However, the nearby Royal Botanic Garden, around half a mile from the route, is a stunning visit, especially in spring when the rhododendrons are out.

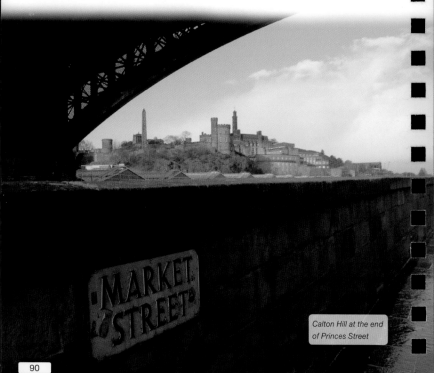

Calton Hill at the end of Princes Street

Traffic free George Street's cycleway

• **Sightseeing** in Edinburgh is a joy, just wander off and enjoy the magnificence of Edinburgh Castle, the awe inspiring St Giles Cathedral, the views from Calton Hill or the extensive collections of the **National Museum** and **Scottish National Portrait Gallery.**
• You don't have to be a politician to visit the **Scottish Parliament** where there are a shop, cafe and exhibition and access to the Debating Chamber itself.
• Perhaps choose something from the wide range of **walking and bus tours** of the city or just go for a ride on the city's excellent new tram line.
• The world famous **Edinburgh International and Fringe festivals** take place in August.

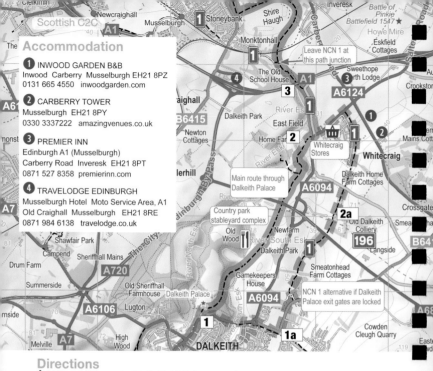

Accommodation

1 INWOOD GARDEN B&B
Inwood Carberry Musselburgh EH21 8PZ
0131 665 4550 inwoodgarden.com

2 CARBERRY TOWER
Musselburgh EH21 8PY
0330 3337222 amazingvenues.co.uk

3 PREMIER INN
Edinburgh A1 (Musselburgh)
Carberry Road Inveresk EH21 8PT
0871 527 8358 premierinn.com

4 TRAVELODGE EDINBURGH
Musselburgh Hotel Moto Service Area, A1
Old Craighall Musselburgh EH21 8RE
0871 984 6138 travelodge.co.uk

Directions

1 At the northern end of Dalkeith High Street you have a choice to make; the Scottish C2C goes straight on here, through the entrance to Dalkeith Country Park. However, check the gates at the far end are open at the entrance kiosk. (If closed see NCN 1 option below)

NCN1 bypass option: For NCN bypass avoiding Dalkeith Country Park swing right in front of the park gates and head out of Dalkeith along Musselburgh Road. Dip over the river and climb to a roundabout, going straight on. In around 0.3km, just past the supermarket, turn left **1a** onto the pavement cycle lane then left by the school to follow NCN1 along a traffic free route. Cross the Pencaitland traffic free route **2a**, following Whitecraig signs. Follow to meet Whitecraig Road and go left, heading through Whitecraig to the roundabout. Go right here to rejoin the main route.

After heading through the gates of the country park at the first split go right. Follow this lovely tarmac estate road past a grandly impressive view of the house. Dip down and through the stableyard area (being developed as a 'family friendly retail, catering and leisure facility' at the time of writing).

Shortly after climbing over the A68 trunk road head right at the first split and curve round to the right to exit the park by Smeaton House B&B **2**.

Go left here and head to a roundabout on the edge of Whitecraig. Turn left, onto Cowpits Road and very shortly take the traffic free River Esk Path down to the left **3** signed as NCN 1 and 76 to Musselburgh and Edinburgh. Shortly NCN1 splits off left over a bridge to Edinburgh.

The Scottish C2C route stays on the same bank of the river, heading straight on. Pass a weir before the path leads onto a road where you head left and shortly to a small wooden bridge on the left **4**.

Head over this bridge and right to meet the A199. Cross at the pedestrian crossing to pick up Eskside West. It's now a case of just following this side of the river (ignore any misleading signage that leads over a bridge towards Musselburgh centre). The road leads to a traffic free path where you join the John Muir Way.

You are finally at the sea! Curve left to follow the lovely seafront promenade path which brings you to Fisherow Harbour, bearing right onto the road here **5**. Meet a busier road and go right. Take care here as you follow the road through Joppa. Take extra care at the junction where the A199 splits off left to Edinburgh **6** (you need to move into the centre of the road - less confident riders might want to negotiate this junction on foot). Brunstane Burn Path option to Edinburgh splits off left shortly before this - see pages 106-7 for more details).

Around 1 km (0.6 miles) after leaving the A199 look to head right, just coming into Portobello, to pick up the lovely red seafront path **7** (you are now also on cycle route 10 to Seafield and Leith).

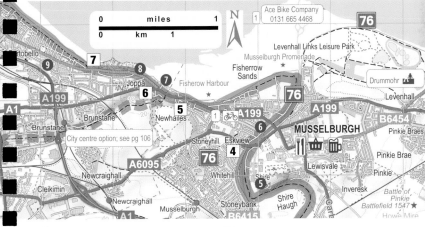

5 EDINBURGH LODGES HOTEL
Carberry Tower Musselburgh EH21 8PY
0131 665 3135 edinburghlodges.com

6 CATHY CAVEN B&B
19, Bridge Street Musselburgh EH21 6AA
0131 665 6560 cathycaven@aol.com

7 MACKENZIE BUNKS
49c Edinburgh Road Musselburgh EH21 6EE
0791 992 1947 mackenziebunks.com

8 ROCKVILLE HOTEL
2 Joppa Pans EH15 2HF
0131 669 5418 rockville.co.uk

9 ARDGARTH GUEST HOUSE
1, St. Mary's Place Portobello EH15 2QF
0131 669 3021 ardgarth.com

DRUMMOHR HOLIDAY PARK
Levenhall Musselburgh EH21 8JS
0131 665 6867 www.drummohr.org
Tent pitches on holiday park

Wheels2Wheels 01721 729756
Mobile bike repair service. Emergency call out service may be available.
Mon-Sat 8am-8pm Cover all of the City of Edinburgh, East Lothian and Midlothian.

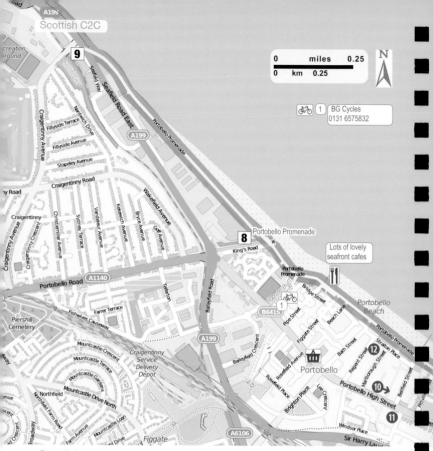

0	miles 0.25
0	km 0.25

🚲 1 BG Cycles
0131 6575832

Portobello Promenade

8 King's Road

Lots of lovely
seafront cafes

Portobello
Promenade

Bridge Street

Portobello
Beach

B6415 1

Pipe Street

Figgate Street

Beach Lane

Portobello Promenade

Bath Street

Stratton Place

Seafield Street

12

Portobello

Regent Street

Marlborough Street

Portobello High Street

10

11

Windsor Place

Sir Harry Lau...

A6106

Figgate

Past all the popular coffee shops and seafront attractions, the seafront path continues (ignore route 10 signs up the impressive looking Kings Road to your left **8**).
When the seafront path eventually climbs to meet the A199 head right along the shared use pavement cycleway **9**. Follow cycle route signs at the crossing to head up Seafield Street **10** and bear right onto tarmac traffic free path, following signs for Leith and Ocean Terminal. Similar signs direct you immediately to the right and an elevated path takes you past a graveyard to the left and over a bridge before dropping down alongside Leith Links themselves. Join the road at Links Gardens and head right along Links Place **11**.

⑩ STRAVEN GUESTHOUSE
3, Brunstane Road North Portobello EH15 2DL
0131 669 5580   stravenguesthouse.com

⑪ ABERCORN GUESTHOUSE
1 Abercorn Terrace Portbello EH15 2DD
0131 669 6139   abercornguesthouse.com

⑫ THE BEACH FRONT GUESTHOUSE
33 Straiton Place Portobello EH15 2BA
0773 249 0016   edinburgh-bb.com/info

There are also several B&B's at Joppa just along the coast from Fisherow, including Abercorn Guesthouse 0131 669 6139, Pearlview Guesthouse 0131 669 8516 and Seabreeze 0131 657 3842.

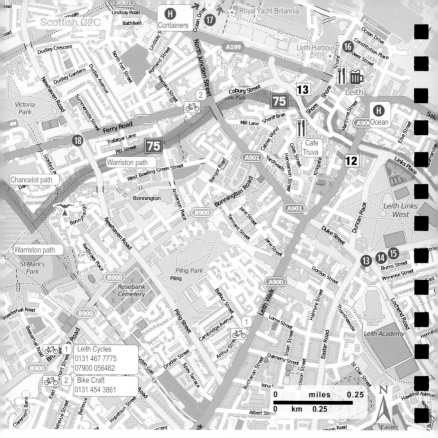

At the major crossroads head straight across **12** (now on NCN 75 and Queen Charlotte Street) and come to a T-junction at Tolbooth Wynd. Turn right onto Water Street, first left onto Burgess Street and left up Shore (Water of Leith on your right now - town centre behind you) to emerge at the the bridge across the Water of Leith. Head right over the bridge and immediately go left **13**, onto the traffic free path, still on NCN 75, with the Water of Leith now on your left.

13 SANDAIG GUEST HOUSE
5 East Hermitage Place Leith Links EH6 8AA
0131 554 7357 sandaigguesthouse.co.uk

14 CULANE HOUSE HOTEL
9 Hermitage Place Leith Links EH6 8AF
0131 554 7331 culanehousehotel.co.uk

15 PARK VIEW HOUSE HOTEL
14 Hermitage Place Leith Links EH6 8AF
0131 554 6206 parkviewhousehotel.co.uk

16 MALMAISON
1 Tower Place Leith EH6 7BZ
0844 693 0652 malmaison.com

17 HOLIDAY INN EXPRESS
Britannia Way Ocean Drive Leith EH6 6JJ
0871 423 4876 holidayinn.com

18 A-HAVEN GUEST HOUSE
180 Ferry Road, Edinburgh EH6 4NS
0131 554 6559 www.a-haven.co.uk

H OCEAN HOSTEL
55 Constitution Street Leith EH6 7BG
0131 553 3003 oceanhostel.com

H CONTAINERS HOSTEL
97 Ocean Drive Leith EH6 6JJ
0208 123 2865 containershostels.com
Budget accommodation only open in summer

Leith's handsome waterfront

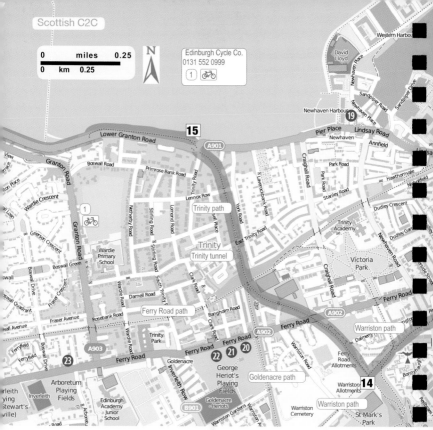

Edinburgh Cycle Co.
0131 552 0999

After 2km / 1.25 miles alongside the Water of Leith pass the Millennium Milepost and ignore the path off down to the left to Balerno. NCN 75 follows the Warriston Path. Very shortly turn right onto Chancelot Path **14** (to Queensferry and Newhaven). Through a tunnel the path drops down to the coast road where you head left **15** onto a promenade path before rejoining the road and heading right.

19 PREMIER INN

51 – 53, Newhaven Place Leith EH6 4TX
0871 527 8360 premierinn.com

20 RAVENSDOWN GUEST HOUSE

248 Ferry Road EH5 3AN
0131 552 5438 ravensdownhouse.com

21 HERIOTT PARK GUEST HOUSE

254 – 256 Ferry Road EH5 3AN
0131 552 3456 heriottpark.co.uk

22 GARFIELD GUEST HOUSE

264 Ferry Road EH5 3AN
0131 552 2369 garfieldguesthouse.co.uk

23 INVERTRUIN B & B

416, Ferry Road Edinburgh EH5 2AD
0131 551 3580 invertruin.co.uk

C2C

Leith, like much of Edinburgh,
has a great traffic free cycle
path network

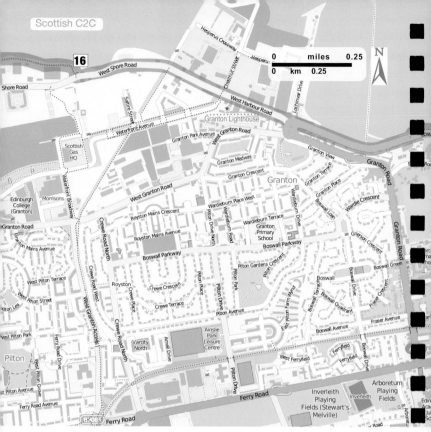

Follow this road through Granton Harbour Estate redevelopment area. Past distant views of the tops of the Forth Bridges you pick up the Silverknowes promenade path over to the right **16**.

After the long sweeping path around Silverknowes the route turns up the River Almond, heading first left **17** to climb steeply through Cramond, passing the Cramond Inn. Bear right onto Cramond Glebe Road and pass Cramond Kirk.

At the main Whitehead Road head right and in just over 1km / 0.6 miles turn right **18**, onto Brae Park Road following NCN 1 signs to drop down on a very quiet residential street. Bend right over the river Almond on a lovely bridge through Cramond conservation area (Cramond Brig Toll).

Climb away from the bridge and by the NCN signs head acutely right through the gate **19** onto the estate track of Dalmeny estate (this is EASY TO MISS; it is actually NCN 76 though it's very easy to carry on past the turning onto NCN 1). For the fully tarmacked, slightly shorter, but less scenic alternative using NCN 1 see opposite above).

24 CRAMOND MILL B&B
Cockle Mill 10 School Brae Cramond EH4 6JN
0131 312 8408   cramondmill.co.uk

25 CRAMOND LODGE
20 Gilmore Place Cramond EH4 6PD
0131 312 8361 07963 347606
cramondlodge.co.uk

EDINBURGH CARAVAN CLUB SITE
35-37 Marine Drive EH4 5EN0
0131 312 6874   caravanclub.co.uk
Tents welcome

Alternative NCN 1 finish avoiding official unsealed NCN76 finish

Whilst not as scenic as the official Scottish C2C finish through Dalmeny Estate, the NCN 1 option does keep you on tarmac all the way to the Forth Rail Bridge and uses fine railpath above South Queensferry and the Forth Estuary.

To take this option don't bear hard right at **19** onto the estate road, but bend gently left and right to come onto the pavement cycle lane alongside the A90 slip road.

Cont. pg 103

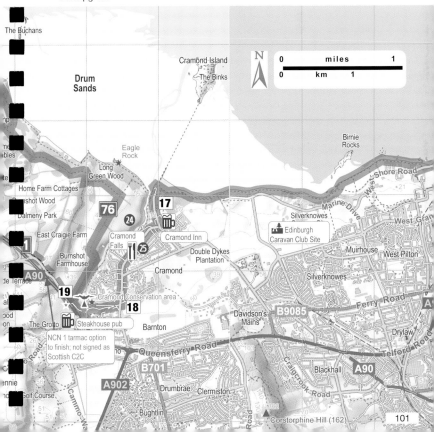

The Buchans

Drum
Sands

Cramond Island
The Binks

Birnie
Rocks

0   miles   1
0   km   1

Eagle
Rock

Long
Green Wood

West Shore Road

Home Farm Cottages

Marine Drive

21

Dalmeny Park

Silverknowes

West Gra

76 **24**

17

Cramond Inn

Edinburgh
Caravan Club Site

West Pilton

East Craigie Farm

Cramond
Falls

25

Muirhouse

Burnshot
Farmhouse

Double Dykes
Plantation

Silverknowes

A90

Cramond

Terrace

19

Cramond Conservation area

18

Davidson's
Mains

Ferry Road

A

The Grotto   Steakhouse pub

B9085

Barnton

Drylaw

NCN 1 tarmac option
to finish; not signed as
Scottish C2C

Queensferry Road

Blackhall

A90

B701

Telford Road

Golf Course

A902

Drumbrae

Clermiston

Cammo Wa

Bughtlin

Corstorphine Hill (162)

Follow clear NCN 76 and John Muir Way signage through the estate at various junctions, with great views of fortified Inchmickery Island at one point. Shortly after this, left then right junctions on smooth tarmac lead you in front of Dalmeny House **20**. After bending right in front of Dalmeny House the track drops down to hug the coast before a lovely section along a wild seashore as the Forth Bridge looms increasingly large. Through a gate the track continues all the way to the road near the base of the bridge and your official finish **21** with the Hawes Inn handily nearby. The comforts of South Queensferry High Street are two minutes along the coast.

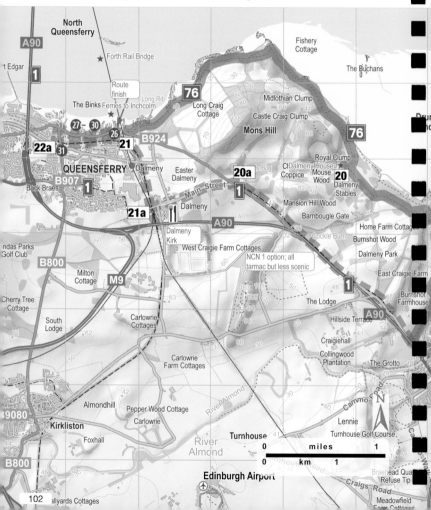

Dalmeny station is little more than a kilometre from the end of the route at South Queensferry and means you can be back at Edinburgh Waverley station in around 20 minutes for quick onward connections.

The Scotrail policy for bikes on trains for local services such as this is that no reservations are necessary but bikes are carried subject to space.

For intercity services their policies are: Caledonian Sleepers between Scotland and London - reservations compulsory. Three cycle spaces per train on Inverness to London sleeper. Six cycle spaces per train on all other sleeper services (including northbound London to Inverness).

A cycle reservation is compulsory on services between Glasgow, Edinburgh and Aberdeen and Glasgow, Edinburgh and Inverness. Cycle reservations are available up to 12 weeks in advance with reservations bookable online at scotrail.co.uk or at staffed stations or via ScotRail Telesales on 0330 303 0111.

26 THE HAWES INN
7, Newhalls Road South Queensferry EH30 9TA
0845 112 6001 innkeeperslodge.com

27 RAVENOUS BEASTIE
15 West Terrace South Queensferry EH30 9LL
0131 319 1447
ravenousbeastie.co.uk

28 NUMBER 18
18 East Terrace South Queensferry, EH30 9HS
0131 331 2407 0796 021 8301
number18.org.uk

29 OROCCO PIER
17 High Street South Queensferry EH30 9PP
0870 118 1664 oroccopier.co.uk
Bed and breakfast & serviced apartment

30 STAGHALL HOTEL
8 High Street South Queensferry EH30 9PP
0131 331 1039

31 PRIORY LODGE
8 The Loan South Queensferry EH30 9NS
0131 331 4345 queensferry.com

Nothing very near the route end (Edinburgh Caravan Club site is some 13km / 8 miles back along the main Scottish C2C route). The nearest site to the route end is at Duloch Hamlet, over the Forth Road Bridge on NCN 1, just north of Inverkeithing, about 9km / 5.5 miles from the official finish. Details are:
CAMPING FIFE
01383 417681 07957 264 805
camping-fife-near-edinburgh.blogspot.co.uk
The following is about 11km / 7 miles west of Edinburgh and does camping and glamping:
LINWATER CARAVAN PARK
East Calder 0131 333 3326   linwater.co.uk
Also note the site up the coast from Musselburgh (see page 93) which you will have passed nearby on the route in.

Alternative NCN 1 finish (continued from page 101)
Keep on the pavement cycle lane for around 3.25km / 2 miles, before crossing the road at the main entrance to Dalmeny House, heading left **20a** on the road to Dalmeny. Head through the village and as the road bends left head straight on, to the cycle signs by the little bridge **21a**. Ignore signs straight on for Round the Forth (this will take you over the road bridge to Inverkeithing and beyond), but head left down the ramp, signed for Dalmeny Station, Queensferry, Kirkliston and Newbridge. Head right at the bottom of the ramp onto this fine railpath and follow it for some 2km / 1.25 miles, as it runs out into a supermarket car park **22a**.
Turn around 180 degrees and at the road (The Loan) go left then first right onto Hopetoun Road which will take you through the centre of South Queensferry and to the Forth Rail Bridge.

EDINBURGH'S CYCLE NETWORK
SHOWING NCN AND LOCAL ROUTES

Scottish C2C

KEY

National cycle network (see numbers below & opposite for route descriptions)

Local routes

Scottish C2C route (yellow highlight)

C2C **C2C** Scottish C2C route - main route bold signing (as on ground) - Edinburgh centre option faint (not signed on the ground)

1 long distance route connecting Dover and the Shetland Islands via the east coast of England and Scotland - 2727km / 1695 miles

75 Leith - Portavadie via Edinburgh & Glasgow. Much of the Edinburgh section folows the water of Leith walkway 183km / 114 miles

76 Kirkcaldy - Dunbar (Round the Forth) heads west and east along the Forth coast but numbered through central Edinburgh 216km / 134 miles

754 Forth & Clyde canal towpath - Bowling, Glasgow, to the Falkirk Wheel then the Union Canal towpath (joining Route 75) into central Edinburgh 90km / 56 miles

105

Edinburgh Centre Option: Brunstane Path to Edinburgh Centre and down to Leith (not signed as Scottish C2C)

The Scottish C2C does not pass through Edinburgh's world-famous centre, though it passes nearby enough to make a visit an easy matter. The National Cycle Network around Edinburgh is particularly dense, taking advantage of the many disused railways and canals to thread its way in and around the city.

Be aware though, that whilst the routes are generally well-signed and maintained as urban cycle routes go, many sections require intricate navigation through estate roads and may add time and distance whilst taking you away from the scenic attractions of the main Scottish C2C route. This guide has selected an option that remains pretty easily navigable and takes you along some of the finest approaches to the city, allowing you to experience this UNESCO World Heritage Site on two wheels.

Pros: Allows for a classic entry into Edinburgh via the wonderful Innocent Railway Path, passing Holyrood Park featuring the magnificent dormant volcano that is Arthur's Seat and onto central Edinburgh's main sights such as The Meadows and Market Street and Princes Street (together the historic heart of the city). There are also the attractions of the atmospheric Innocent Tunnel and the great segregated, continental-style traffic free path through the very heart of Edinburgh along George Street.

Cons: Bypasses the lovely section of the main Scottish C2C route along Portobello promenade. Adds around a mile and a half to your route and involves a rather tricky section along numerous central streets between the Innocent Tunnel and The Meadows and some fairly heavily trafficked streets between Meadow Walk and George Street.

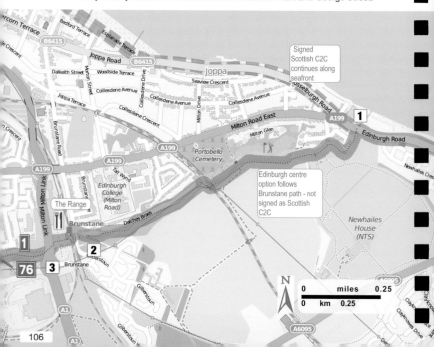

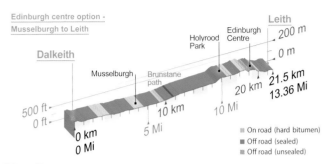

Edinburgh centre option -
Musselburgh to Leith

Directions

After leaving Fisherow and joining the main road you pass out of East Lothian and
see the sign telling you you're now in Edinburgh City; very shortly look out for a path
alongside Brunstane Burn **1** (**easy to miss** but signed Brunstane Burn path) over to the
left. Cross over the burn and in Brunstane Mill Park head across a junction and simply
follow the path for some 1.5km / nearly 1 mile and meet a road **2**. Head right and at
the junction head across the road to cross the railway line on the bridge (an easy push
over the stepped ramps). Head straight on through the supermarket carpark to a path
junction. Head left, signed Bingham, under the main road **3**. Go right at two splits in
quick succession, following NCN1 signs.

This pleasant tarmac path takes you above Magdalene Glen down to the left and then
across a main road **4**. Follow the path across the open green area, bending right away
from the bridge and across the path crossroads, all the while following NCN1 signs
towards Edinburgh and Duddingston.

107

Passing out of Jewel Park in Bingham soon cross another road, picking up the old Innocent Railway **5**, following signs for City Centre and St Leonards. Immediately pass over the old iron bridge then pass along the lovely section close by Holyrood Park. Through the tunnel head straight on, through a small housing area and onto Hermits Croft, bearing right onto a traffic free section at the end. Head left onto the cobbles of St Leonards Lane **6** then head diagonally across St Leonards Street onto Rankeillor Street (still on NCN1). Across Clerk Street go down Gifford Park passageway and left onto Buccleuch Street **7** then very shortly right onto the path that is North Meadow Walk.

Keep hard right to follow this lovely path past tennis courts as the beautiful parkland of The Meadows opens out to your left. Very shortly head right by the Sustrans Milepost **8**, up the cycle lane along Middle Meadow Walk. At the end of the cycle lane rejoin the traffic straight ahead (Forrest Road) and follow your nose to dip down over George IV Bridge which then meets Lawnmarket (Royal Mile) at a crossroads **9**. Head straight across onto Bank Street, bending left and descending onto the Mound with fantastic views on this classic entrance into the heart of Edinburgh.

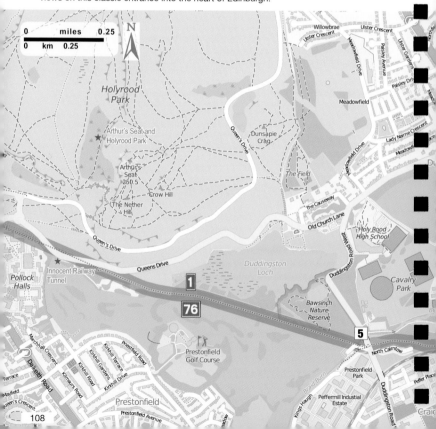

Wiggle right and left across Princes Street, up Hanover Street **10**. Meet George Street and right onto the excellent segregated cycle lane, leaving NCN1 for NCN75. This leads to the impressive St Andrew Square with its towering Melville Monument.

View from Princes Street towards Arthur's Seat

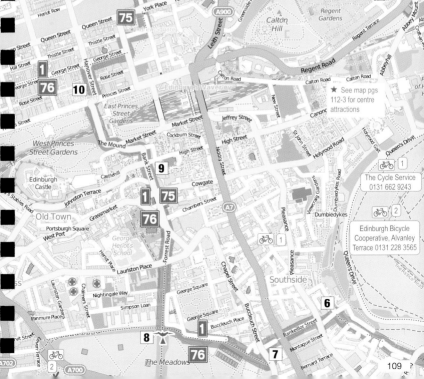

The Cycle Service
0131 662 9243

Edinburgh Bicycle
Cooperative, Alvanley
Terrace 0131 228 3565

★ See map pgs
112-3 for centre
attractions

Accommodation cont. see overleaf for map entries

1 MERCURE HOTEL
Princes Street EH2 2DG
0207 660 8104 mercure.com

2 GRASSMARKET HOTEL
94 – 96, Grassmarket EH1 2JR
0131 220 2299 thegrassmarkethotel.co.uk

3 THE GEORGE HOTEL
19 – 21, George Street EH2 2PB
0844 854 2910 thegeorgehoteledinburgh.co.uk

4 IBIS STYLES HOTEL
19, St. Andrew Square EH2 1HU
0131 292 0200 accorhotels.com

5 INCHGROVE HOUSE
17a Abercromby Place EH3 6LB
0131 225 4343 inchgrovehouse.co.uk

6 THE GUEST ROOM B & B
31a Nelson Street EH3 6LJ
0131 556 4798 theguestroom.co.uk

7 CARAVEL GUEST HOUSE
30 London Street EH3 6NA
0131 556 4444 caravelhouse.com

8 RAMSAY'S B & B
25, East London Street EH7 4BN
0131 557 5917
ramsaysbedandbreakfastedinburgh.com

T TRAVELODGES
Meuse Lane EH2 2BY
0871 559 1855

17 Waterloo Place EH1 3BG
0871 984 6445

37 – 43, Rose Street EH2 2NH
0871 984 6441

www.travelodge.co.uk

H CASTLE ROCK HOSTEL
15 Johnston Terrace EH1 2PW
0131 225 9666 castlerockedinburgh.com
Bike storage

H EDINBURGH CENTRAL YOUTH HOSTEL
(SYHA)
9 Haddington Place EH7 4AL
0131 524 2090 syha.org.uk
Bike storage and chargeable left luggage

H HAGGIS HOSTELS
5/3 West Register Street EH2 2AA
0131 557 0036 haggishostels.co.uk
2 night minimum stay on Sats and during some
events Secure bike storage at Waverley station

H LIGHT HOUSE HOSTELS
20 Gilmore Place Edinburgh EH3 9NQ
07910 834 785
lighthousehostel.co.uk
Min stay periods at some times

*Edinburgh's New Town,
an architectural gem*

The city centre route heads through Rodney Street Tunnel on its way to rejoin the main Scottish C2C route

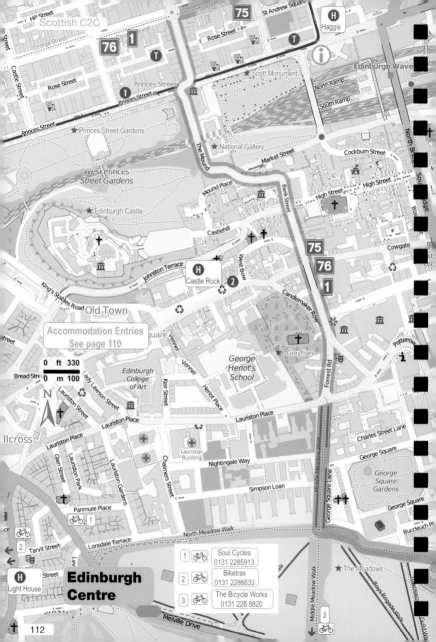

Scottish C2C

75 St Andrew Square

76 **1** George Street

H Haggis

Edinburgh Wave

Rose Street

T

T

Princes Street

Scott Monument

North Ramp

South Ramp

Princes Street Gardens

★ Princes Street Gardens

National Gallery

★ The Mound

Market Street

Cockburn Street

North Bridge

West Princes Street Gardens

★ Edinburgh Castle

Mound Place

Bank Street

High Street

High Street

South Bridge

Castlehill

Castlehill

Cowgate

H Castle Rock **2**

Johnston Terrace

West Bow

75

76

1

Candlemaker Row

King's Stables Road

Old Town

**Accommodation Entries
See page 110**

Vennel

Vennel

Keir Street

Heriot Place

George Heriot's School

Greyfriars

Forrest Rd

Potterrow

i

0 ft 330
0 m 100

Bread Street

Lady Lawson Street

Edinburgh College of Art

Lauriston Street

Lauriston Place

Lauriston Place

Lauriston Place

Charles Street Lane

George Square

Ilcross

Lauriston Place

Chalmers Street

Lauriston Building

Nightingale Way

Lauriston Place

George Square

Glen Street

Lauriston Park

Lauriston Gardens

Simpson Loan

Middle Meadow Walk

George Square Lane

George Square Gardens

George Square

Buccleuch Pl

Panmure Place

1

North Meadow Walk

2 Tarvit Street

Lonsdale Terrace

Lev

H
Light House Street

Edinburgh Centre

★ The Meadows

Boys' Brigade Walk

3

Melville Drive

1	🚲	Soul Cycles 0131 2285913
2	🚲	Biketrax 0131 2286633
3	🚲	The Bicycle Works 0131 228 8820

Bear left onto pavement cycle lane down North St Andrew Street and use the main road crossing **11** onto Dublin Street. Descend steeply to curve across Drummond Place and down Scotland Street. Here the cycle signs direct you down the cycle path into King George V Park **12**. Bend right and left to go through Rodney Street Tunnel to join the Warriston Path, passing Tesco's and crossing Water of Leith.

Soon after Goldenacre Path joins from the left the main Scottish C2C route heads off left along the Chancelot Path (see page 96). If you head straight on you can visit Leith centre, just 5 minutes ride down the Water of Leith, coming back up the same riverside path to follow the Scottish C2C along the coast (again see page 94).

i **Edinburgh** 3 Princes Street 0131 473 3868 visitscotland.com

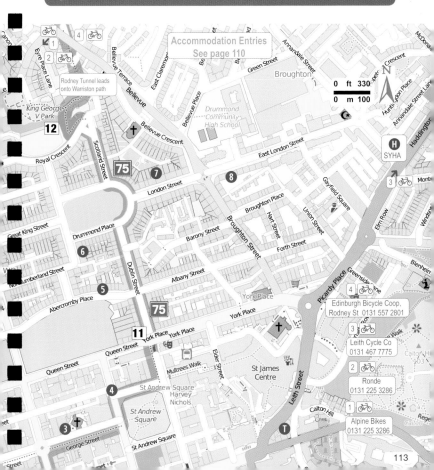

Appendix I Useful websites

cyclingscotland.org
'Cycling Scotland is the national cycle training, promotion, events and engineering organisation for Scotland'

visitscotland.com

innertubemap.com

visitmidlothian.org.uk

edinburgh.gov.uk
A series of detailed downloadable route maps

spokes.org.uk
Edinburgh's excellent cycle lobby group

cyclingdumfries.wordpress.com

laid-back-bikes.scot
Specialist in recumbent and folding bikes. Shop just south of The Meadows.

scottishcyclingmag.co.uk
Free magazine in both digital and print form

The Scottish C2C along Portobello promenade

Appendix II   Signed Scottish long distance cycle routes

Route	Details	Length
Border Loop	Circular tour taking in Kelso, Hawick, Peebles, Innerleithen, Melrose, Duns and Coldstream.	402km 250 miles
National Cycle Network Route 1 in Scotland	From the English border via Edinburgh, Aberdeen and Inverness through the Orkneys and across the Shetlands. Includes the Scottish section of the Coast and Castles.	Well over 1100km Around 700 miles
National Cycle Network Route 7	Carlisle to Inverness taking in Galloway Forest Park and the Loch Lomond and Trossachs National Parks.	692km 430 miles
Forth and Clyde	Effectively an NCN coast to coast from Gourock to Glasgow and Edinburgh (via Falkirk on a northern option or Livingston to the south).	150 km 93 miles
The Tweed Cycle Way	Runs through the Scottish Borders between Biggar and Berwick-upon-Tweed.	153km 95 miles
Round the Forth route	Runs from Edinburgh to Kirkcaldy via Stirling and includes the Salmon Run route following the River Tay between Dundee and Pitlochry. Also includes NCN 1 to Dunbar and to Berwick-upon-Tweed in England.	215km 134 miles
Caledonian Way	Campbeltown to Inverness. Much of it is complete and that which isn't can be cycled using detours. The entire route - on and off road - being planned to be finished in 2016.	367km 228 miles

Appendix III Other signed UK coast to coast routes

Route	From	Length
Belfast to Ballyshannon	Via Portadown, Omagh & Enniskillen	389km / 242 miles
C2C	Whitehaven or Workington to Tynemouth or Sunderland	225km / 140 miles
Devon Coast to Coast	Ilfracombe to Plymouth	160km / 100 miles
Hadrian's Cycleway	Ravenglass to South Shields	280km / 174 miles
Lon Las Cymru	Holyhead to Cardiff or Chepstow	502km / 312 miles
Reivers Route	Tynemouth to Whitehaven (return C2C)	277km / 172 miles
Trans Pennine Trail (TPT)	Southport to Hornsea - around 60% traffic free	333km / 208 miles
Walney to Wear	Walney Island, Cumbria to Sunderland or Whitby	243km / 151 miles
Way of the Roses	Morecambe to Bridlington	273km / 170 miles

Coast to Coast route guides from

EXCELLENT BOOKS

www.excellentbooks.co.uk

Ultimate C2C Guide

- 144 pages
- Maps / attractions
- Directions
- Accommodation
- Food & Drink

TPT Visitor Guide
(to accompany official maps)

- 112 pages
- Outline maps
- Accommodation
- Food & Drink

Ultimate Devon Coast to Coast Guide

- 80 pages
- Maps / attractions
- Directions
- Accommodation
- Food & Drink

...or plan your own with the **Ultimate UK Cycle Route Planner** The whole of the UK's signed cycle routes mapped on one sheet

Organised and supported trips on this Scottish
Coast to Coast route and on the original C2C at

chain-events.co.uk

David Gray has vast experience of running
adventures and trips on routes throughout the UK
and will be happy to put together a trip for you and
your friends, family, team-mates, work colleagues,
charity riders or indeed just about any cycling group

Options for camping or B&B, transport to start and
finish, luggage carriage and mechanical support
throughout by one of the founders of the original C2C

Interchangeable monkii System

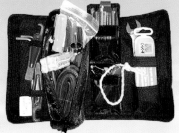

monkii V wedge

- ◆ Clip it on. Clip it off
- ◆ For your tools and repair essentials
- ◆ Tough construction
- ◆ 1 x large zipped pocket, 2 x hook and loop pockets, 4 x elastic holders
- ◆ Fill it. Roll it (strong hook & loop closure)

*Tools shown for display purposes only

monkii clip

- ◆ Carry a water bottle on your Brompton or Strida
- ◆ Doesn't interfere with the fold
- ◆ Also fits any round 25mm-38mm frame, fork, seat, H/B post
- ◆ monkii cage, monkii V wedge, monkii mono, gorilla cage all fit the monkii clip

monkii cage

- ◆ Clip it on. Clip it off
- ◆ Carry a bottle / Thermos from 0.5L to 1.5L
- ◆ Flexible to carry narrow or wide containers
- ◆ Tough construction
- ◆ Won't scratch your containers

⌨ cyclemiles.co.uk

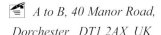

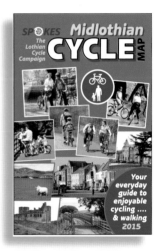

Commute, tour & explore
with our range of folding bicycles

Rhino
'Wild thing'

Chameleon
'Iconic folding road bike'

Joey
'All rounder'

Helios

Morpheus

You can also hire our bikes

www.circecycles.com
+44 (0)1954 782020

C2C

www.uppertweed
railwaypaths.org.uk